HAUNTED
KINGSPORT

HAUNTED KINGSPORT

GHOSTS OF TRI-CITY TENNESSEE

PETE DYKES

Haunted America

Published by Haunted America
A Division of The History Press
Charleston, SC 29403
www.historypress.net

Illustrations were drawn by the author or reprinted from art previously used in his
newspaper columns in the *Daily News* of Kingsport.

First published 2008

Manufactured in the United States

ISBN 978.1.59629.494.3

Library of Congress Cataloging-in-Publication Data

Dykes, Pete.
Haunted Kingsport : ghosts of Tri-City Tennessee / Pete Dykes.
p. cm.
ISBN 978-1-59629-494-3
1. Ghosts--Tennessee--Kingsport. 2. Haunted places--Tennessee--Kingsport. I. Title.
BF1472.U6D95 2008
133.109768'95--dc22
2008041952

CONTENTS

UNSEEN FORCE

You may have driven past the old house near Indian Springs many times without noticing anything odd, but people stopped living there decades ago because of the strange happenings inside.

Years ago, a man and his wife lived there. They had no children, and when the wife's younger brother and his bride fell on hard times because the young man lost his job, they let the younger couple move in with them.

The new couple was given an upstairs room, just at the head of the staircase, while the other tenants continued to sleep in their usual bedroom, on the ground floor of the building.

In a short while, the young couple in the upstairs bedroom began to hear strange noises in the night.

The door to the room seemed to have a habit of clicking loose and swinging open, making a creepy squeaking noise. This would occur several times during the night.

The young man tried to latch the door shut, but it would still open. He tried tying it, but the result was the same. Several times during the night, the squeaking noise would sound and the door would click open, sounding very much as if someone was opening the door and walking in.

The young couple sat up to watch, and the door would open, as if to admit somebody, then click closed again, all by itself.

They began to be concerned and fearful over this strange happening, although they continued to sleep in the room.

But times were hard, and the older man soon lost his job as well.

Unable to continue to pay the rent, he and his wife decided to move out.

The younger couple had no choice. They couldn't pay the rent either, so they decided to pack up and move out again, and go live with the young man's parents.

The young man's uncle came to help them move.

They had loaded up about everything but a final "scrap load"—a few old things they didn't really need but hated to leave behind, and had carried that out to the wagon when they heard a loud noise that caused them to pause.

It sounded like someone had thrown down a load of boards on the upstairs floor.

"What in the world was that?" the uncle asked.

"I don't know," was the reply.

They raced back upstairs to find out what had made the noise, but there was nothing to be seen. The bare room was vacant, no sign of anything that could have caused such a commotion.

"I'm glad to be leaving here," the young bride said.

"There's something wrong about this old house."

Later, another family moved in. But they didn't stay there long.

One night, the wife said, she heard the door open, and somebody walking across the floor and up the stairs. She jumped up to see who was there, but saw only the empty, dark hallway. She awakened her husband and he searched the house, but could find no trace of any intruder.

The next night, both husband and wife were startled out of their sleep by the sound of footsteps on the stairs. The door of the room suddenly opened, and the steps move across the floor.

The husband quickly struck a match and lit a lamp, but no one was there.

They moved out the next day, and the old house has remained vacant since.

HENLEY'S HAUNTED HOUSE

The Henley farm consisted of more than a hundred acres of land, part of it covered with a thick woodland, choked and tangled with a heavy growth of underbrush.

In the midst of this thorny, tangled growth stood an old, dilapidated and decaying house. No one had lived there for many years. In fact, not even Grandma Simms, the oldest resident of the entire community, could recall anyone ever having been in residence there. The old house just stood there, rotting away, in the middle of the thick, tangled woods, occupied only by rats, mice and an opossum or two.

Tales had grown up about the old house—scary, chilling, spooky tales of ghosts and terror, yarns and stories that would literally make your hair stand on end when you heard them.

But, so far as anyone knew for sure, they were just tales, figments of someone's imagination, sparked by eerie sounds on a dank, dark night.

Among the older boys of the neighborhood, the rotting old structure became known as Henley's Haunted House, and the oft-repeated dare or challenge was to spend a night within its creaking walls.

One boy—Fred, his name was—decided to take the dare and accept the challenge.

"I am going to spend the night in Henley's Haunted House," he declared. "Will any one of you fellows go with me?"

Billy couldn't go; he had a cold.

Joe had too much homework to do.

Chad's mother was going to change the bed sheets, and needed him to stay home and help her with the work.

Jackie had too much work to do, helping his father feed the farm stock and all.

There were other excuses, too, some of them more believable than others.

Fred, however, was determined to go through with his announced intentions. With a companion or alone, he would spend a night in Henley's Haunted House.

So, packing up the necessities and needs he felt he required, Fred set out for his declared destination.

He took along half a box of Twinkies, a couple of Moon Pies, two bologna and cheese sandwiches, a Snickers bar and a two-liter bottle of Gatorade, all packed up nicely in his old Boy Scout knapsack.

Fred also took along his flashlight, pocketknife and his BB pistol, just in case one of them might be needed.

The tangled trail through the woods was difficult to travel, and Fred's progress was slow. In some places, he had to break down brush and brambles just to get through. The old pathway was so grown up with weeds, briars and brush that he found he could make better time by hacking his way through the woodland itself, avoiding the path and its barricade of thorns.

At last, after a good bit of trouble and a lot of work, Fred arrived at the old house. The sunset filtering through the shadows of the trees made a kind of pink glow around the dilapidated wreck, and heavy wisps of mist floated around the gloomy, slanting, shackled walls, giving the place an eerie, ghostly appearance that made Fred's heart beat faster in spite of his brave resolve.

The creaking door shrieked on its rusty hinges as Fred pulled it open. His heart almost stopped with terror at the sudden sound.

But Fred swallowed hard, took a deep breath and pushed his way inside.

The old hallway was a wreck, with ancient staircase steps broken and sagging down, decaying with age, half of them already collapsed and gone, leaving a gaping hole halfway up the ramshackle affair. The broken banister lay across the darkened, empty space, a tiny bridge across the gulf between the treads.

Fred made his way into the first big room, just off the rubble-filled hallway.

A wide old stone fireplace and hearth occupied most of one wall, leaning crazily toward the center of the room as if it might decide to pitch forward at any time and stretch prone on the creaking floor.

There were broken windows on one side of the room, and a tall old door in the center of another wall.

Part of the ceiling had already fallen down, and Fred looked up through the yawning hole toward the second floor, where sagging floor beams were weighted down with age and exhaustion.

"Golly," Fred said softly to himself. "This place *is* creepy."

He slipped out of his backpack and set it carefully on the stone hearth.

"Maybe I better build a fire," he decided.

There was plenty of scrap wood already in the room, most of it so old and decayed that it was perfect for kindling tinder. Fred broke up a few pieces of it and arranged them carefully in the fireplace. He struck a match, and soon had a cheery little fire burning, sending its flickering light dancing among the deep gloomy shadows of the twilight-shrouded room.

"This won't be so bad," Fred told himself, unwrapping a Moon Pie and chomping down on it between gulps of Gatorade.

"There's nothing here to be afraid of."

Suddenly, the air seemed to split with a horrible, shrieking, wailing, mournful sound!

Fred felt cold chills run up his backbone and grab his heart. He choked on the Gatorade and coughed, spewing a mouthful of the liquid across the shadowy room.

The mournful wailing was right outside, near the shattered windows across the room.

Fred's heart almost stopped, and then it beat harder than ever before.

For a long minute, the boy stood as if frozen, then he grabbed the knapsack and plunged his way through the door, across the hallway and outside.

Fred didn't have a bit of trouble getting back through the tangled woods. Oh, he got a few cuts and scratches from brush and brambles here and there, but he made it all the way back to the county road in no time flat.

Back at the old house, a tiny screech owl flapped its wings and flew through a broken window to a favorite perch in the rotting ceiling beams above its nest.

Fred, halfway home, suddenly realized that his friends would all laugh at him for running away from the haunted house.

He spent the night in Simpson's barn, enjoying his Gatorade, sandwiches, Twinkies and Moon Pies in the safe, sturdy, comfortable surroundings of the haymow.

He never told about running away; he only described, with the accuracy of detail that could only come from personal observation, the appearance of the old house and its rotting interior.

Fred became a sort of hero to the other boys, one to be looked up to for his bravery and courage, and envied for his gall.

But he never, ever again attempted to spend a night in Henley's Haunted House.

DEATH CROWNS ON THE PILLOW

The back-road country of the southern Appalachians has its own superstitions and native lore that may well be different from any other you can find in other parts of the country or world.

But some of the beliefs are strongly held to, at least by the small and shrinking percentage of residents who cling to the old tenets that their parents and grandparents took great stock in.

There are "signs" and "omens," once widely recognized and held as harbingers of what was to be—forbidden places and things that must be avoided at all cost, and certain words and names that must never be spoken aloud.

Death Crowns were one of the strongly held beliefs only a few years ago. Whether such items exist now or have ever done so, this writer can only speak from personal experience and say that he has never seen one. But there are strange things under heaven that no man can explain.

When little Lillybelle Maggard died, her parents were saddened to the point of near desperation.

"I'll never get over this," Celia Ann said.

Her husband, Lilburn, tried to be sympathetic, but he was too deeply hurt and sorrowed himself to be much comfort.

"She's with the angels now," was the best he could offer. "No more suffering nor pain will she have to bear."

"I know all that Lilburn," Celia Ann said, "but I miss my little girl so much. She was such a treasure for an eight year old."

"I miss her too," Lilburn said. "I don't know why she was took."

Celia Ann decided to be brave and clean up the dead child's room.

"If I don't do it now," she wisely said, "it'll never get done, and it'll be harder to do every day I put it off."

So, with determination and tearful eyes, she set about the duties of removing the girl's clothes and personal things. It was the feather pillow that gave birth to this tale.

"The poor thing sweated so much at the last," Celia Ann said, "She even soaked the pillow. I'm going to just empty it out, and burn the feathers." That's when she found the "crown."

A tiny ring of feathers, just large enough to cover a silver dollar, clung together when the pillow case was emptied out.

"Lilburn, come here and look at this," Celia Ann called. "I never seen anything like it before."

Lilburn came and looked.

"Why," he said, "It's a death crown!"

He then explained to his wife the belief held by many mountain people that when a righteous person died, a crown could be found in the pillow that had supported their head—a mute testimony that a crown of glory had been given to them in heaven.

"It's a sign that they went to heaven," Lilburn said. "So you can know that Lillybelle is with Jesus and God now, and is alright."

Celia Ann felt tears start to trickle down her cheeks, and she looked quickly at Lilburn. He, too, was crying. Tears of sadness, yet tears of joy.

"I'm going to save it!" Celia Ann exclaimed, and hurried off to get a box.

She carefully placed the crown in a shoe box, and stored it away in her chest, a memento of the tiny and innocent life that had been taken away from them. Some weeks passed before the crown in the shoe box came to mind again.

"I want to show you something," Celia Ann said to her neighbor, Mrs. Fugate. "We found this perfect little crown in the pillow my Lillybelle died on, and I saved it."

She opened the shoe box and gasped in surprise. The tiny crown had grown! It was now large enough to cover a saucer, rather than the tiny silver dollar size it had been when she tucked it away. Lilburn was puzzled, too.

"I never seen anything like that," he said.

There seemed to be a layer of downy fuzz about the base of the crown, as if it had fallen off all around and was now knitting to the outer edges and growing into new, fresh feathers, much like how the down of new feathers form and grow on a goose or duck! Mrs. Fugate saw the feather crown and heard their statements, but, having not seen the original article before it was stored away, could not say whether or not it had grown.

For some time, Lilburn and Celia Ann marveled at the strange event. But as the shock wore off, they decided to store the crown away again and see what it might be at a future time. A month went by before they took it out to look at it again. The crown was bigger than before! Now, it had grown until the edges of it touched the inside walls of the shoe box! Lilburn hurried off to get Mrs. Fugate to come and see this marvel of a growing feather crown.

"Well I swan!" the good woman cried when she viewed the object. "It's really grown! What do you think about that?"

Neither Celia Ann or Lilburn could answer. They simply did not know what to think. A larger box was found, one that offered room for more growth. Up and down the holler and across the hill the story was told. Neighbors came from miles away to see the "crown." Lilburn became concerned that someone might drop the box and damage its precious contents.

"We're a-puttin' it away again," he said firmly. "Y'all can come back in three months when we open it up again, and see if it's still growin'."

A day was agreed upon when the box would again be brought out and opened, and anticipation sat impatiently on the entire community. A week or so before the "showing" day, Celia Ann got word that her oldest sister had died. She and Lilburn hurried off, afoot, to the ten-mile-distant home of bereavement, and were there for the three-day wake, funeral and burial.

"She was a good woman," Lilburn said. "You reckon there was a death crown in her pillow?"

"She didn't die in bed," Celia Ann replied. "She fell over dead in the kitchen. Had a heart attack, the doctor said. She didn't have no death crown, because her head wasn't on no pillow when she died. That don't mean she didn't go to heaven, though."

"I reckon you're right," Lilburn agreed. "But I'm sure glad we got us one!"

They had made the long trek home in time to arrive at their house just before the sun set.

"Let's get that Death Crown out and look at it again," Lilburn said.

Celia Ann agreed. But a minute later, she came rushing back into the room.

"It's GONE!" she cried. "Box and all! It's just gone!"

Did someone break in and take the Death Crown away, storage box and all? Celia Ann and Lilburn never did find out. And the growing Death Crown was never seen again.

But it was heard about, for the story was told and retold throughout the Appalachians, and may be yet, for all I know. Feather pillows have gone the way of butter churns and spinning wheels, replaced in most homes by foam rubber or other hypoallergenic substances and materials for modern comfort.

But deep in the back-road country, where local traditions and family folklore yet abound, some folks remain quick to examine the death pillow of a family member for that tangible proof that the departed soul has indeed found its home and won a crown of its own.

AMOS'S HOLLOW

A few miles east of Dungannon, Virginia, on the old Fincastle Turnpike, there's a dim and dismal spot, dark and gloomy even at midday, where a little stream runs between two steep hills.

There is usually a heavy growth of buckeye, poplar, basswood and oak covering the steep ridges that makes the shadows even gloomier. That spot has been called Amos's Hollow for as long as anyone now living can recall, but few people can tell how and why the place was so designated.

Amos Turner was a prosperous keg maker during the early days of the War Between the States. As such, his services were much in demand, both by local citizens and, later, by the growing contingent of Confederate army folk stationed nearby.

So much false and misleading information has been written about the so-called "Civil" War that it is difficult to understand just what did take place in many instances, and motivation for the fighting is one of those misreported areas. Although some would have you believe that the war was fought to free slaves, such was not the case at all. The slaves were freed, it is true, by Lincoln's Emancipation Proclamation, but that came only in the autumn of 1862, when the war was far into its second year. The slaves who were freed were only from those states that had rebelled. The proclamation did not apply to those held by the states that had remained in the Union!

When he heard earlier of threats of secession, the president ordered Federal troops into Virginia, which considered the act an invasion of its sovereign territory. Then South Carolina's tempers flared when Federal gunboats continued to supply both additional troops and ammunition to Fort Sumter,

and, having their orders to evacuate the fort and its threat to Charleston ignored, the Confederates rashly opened fire, giving the Federals the excuse they needed to attempt to ravish and destroy the South.

With those facts in evidence, it is easier to understand how and why Amos Turner ran into trouble. Amos was an abolitionist who believed from the start that slavery was a sin and should not be condoned. He had read the *Emancipator*, that antislavery paper printed in Jonesborough, Tennessee, and he even concurred with the more violent demands. And so it was that when, after Lincoln "freed" the slaves, giving no compensation at all to their owners, Amos Turner's defense of the action put him at odds with many of his neighbors.

Although there had been several Federal sympathizers in the area, most of them had gone north, either to join the Yankee forces or to find safer living conditions. By the early days of 1863, most of what is now southeastern Virginia was firmly under Confederate control.

Amos's outspokenness first cost him his keg-making business. The Confederate army would not deal with any man who seemed to offer opposition in any form. By insisting that no man had the right to own another, Amos put many of his former friends and neighbors firmly in the ranks of his enemies. True, very few of them, if any, owned slaves; but some of them had relatives who did, and taking away such property without compensation, as the Federals were doing, just didn't sit well with their Appalachian pride. Then came conscription. The Confederate army, desperate for more "cannon fodder," began taking any men they could find into their ranks, or eliminating them as possible future enemies.

"I'll not fight and kill to help keep slaves for the big plantation owners," Amos declared. "I don't believe in killing, any more than slavery, so I won't join the Federals, either."

But such a noble attitude did little to improve his chance of survival in a war-torn world. When the Confederate cavalry came—a full company of them, armed and well trained—to seek out any "malingers," Amos realized that he was in trouble.

"I'll take to the hills, and hide out until this war is over," he said.

And, with that, he sent his family away to live with a Northern relative while he himself took refuge in the dismal little hollow that has since born his name. Planning to hide out and live off the land, Amos managed to find a small cave for shelter, stocking it with a few necessary supplies. One day, however, the soldiers came, searching from tree to tree even in the miserable little refuge. Amos, routed from his hiding place, tried to run.

"Halt!" cried a sergeant. "Halt, or I'll shoot!"

Amos didn't halt. They left his body just lying there, where it had fallen. Weeks later, buzzards circling over the trees caused someone to investigate, and the rotting body was discovered. Well, he had been a neighbor, and he was dead now and gone. So it fell to a group of local folks to bury his remains. A buckeye log was split and troughed out, half for a coffin and the other half for a lid. Amos was buried where he had fallen, in the dark and dismal hollow beside the little creek.

But strangely enough, the following year, the little grave mound was profusely decorated with wildflowers from the woods. Folks assumed some of Amos's relatives had come to decorate the grave. But the effort was continued year after year, and none of his relations were ever heard about in the area. At long last, seeds from the many wildflowers that had graced the grave site took root, and a little garden of wildflowers has grown there ever since. Some say the flowers were placed by former slaves in the area who knew of Amos's refusal to join the Southern ranks, thinking that his goal may have been to help make them free.

Others think children in the neighborhood may have decorated the grave out of pity. No one knows for sure. But the hollow still bears his name, and the wildflowers still bloom each spring.

FOLKS FEARED FELINES COULD CAUSE "GO-BACKS"

Years ago, throughout the Appalachians, many people had a strong belief that certain cats would suck the breath from growing children, resulting in stunting the child's physical and mental growth and sometimes even resulting in death.

Indeed, many children grew ill with what was then called "the go-backs," and their health failed, causing them to dwindle away and lose weight, becoming frail and listless.

Although modern medicine and good nutrition might well have cured many a "go-back" patient, at the time, the illness was often blamed on the family cat.

Old tales from our area contain a lot of folklore concerning breath-sucking cats. Decades ago, I jotted down notes from an interview with an elderly woman who resided high on Bays Mountain.

I rec'lect hearing my Pa tell about his little sister. I can't remember what her name might have been, she died when my pa was jist a boy, and I don't know as I ever hear him say it. But he said they had an old gray cat that stayed around the house, and the first thing they knowed, the little girl had made friends with it.

That ol' cat got to where it would follow her around all the time, and would tag along wherever she went.

She was only four or five years old, and thought the cat was great fun. It got to where it wanted her to pick it up and hold it like a baby, and she done that a lot, too.

Well, they didn't pay much attention, but after a while they noticed that the little girl was a-fallin off, and losing weight.

"I'm afraid she's got the go-backs!" Pa's Ma said.

Well, as soon as they found out that somethin' was wrong with the girl, they started trying to doctor her up some.

They gave her rattleweed tea and sassafras brew, and tried other remedies they knowed about on her, but none of them done any good. The girl just kept a-wastin' away.

She started to get pale and listless, and she didn't have any appetite at all hardly.

All the while, that old gray cat would sit right in front on the little girl's bed from daylight till dark.

At night, they'd hear him purrin' and going on, and when they'd get up to look, that ol' cat would be stretched out right on that little girl's breast, flat on its belly, with its mouth right up against the child's mouth in a kind of suckin' manner and its forepaws just a-paddin' up and down!

They knowed right then what was the matter with the child. That ol' cat was sucking her breath and a-sappin' the very life out of her! They didn't know what to do.

They had tried all the remedies they knowed about, so they finally taken her to a doctor to see if he could cure her. Well, he gave her some pills and such, but they didn't do any more for her than the teas and such had.

It's bad luck to kill a cat. Everybody knows that. So Grand Ma wouldn't let Pa kill the old cat, for fear it would bring even more calamities down on them.

So Pa made a wooden box, and they put the cat in it and shut it up in it. That old cat didn't like that one bit and wouldn't eat, and so it didn't do no good at all.

Granny, when she milked the cows, would give it some milk to drink, and Pa and his brothers would crumble up bread crumbs and put in the box for him, but the cat wouldn't touch nothing at all.

That old cat would just kind of turn its head toward where the little sick girl's bed was and make that funny kind of a-sucking noise in that direction! Well, the little girl died that night. When they went to look at the cat in the box the next morning, it was dead, too.

I reckon the girl and the cat both must have died just about the same time. I'll tell you one thing. I never let no cats come in my house and get a chance to suck the breath out of my young'ns when they was small.

Law, law. There's strange things in this old world. And that story is true, too, because my Pa told me it, and he wouldn't never tell no lie.

DEVIL CAT

According to an old tale I heard recently, a multiple-murder case was once solved because of the intervention of a large black cat. Some folks believed the devil possessed the feline, using its body to house and mask his own terrifying spirit. Others say the animal was created solely to seek out justice and bring guilt upon the perpetrators of unspeakable evil deeds.

Here are the facts, as told to me. Judge it for yourself.

Many years ago, a woman lived near our town, a woman of bad reputation. She was never married, but had a whole houseful of children, four of them, sired, it was said, by a variety of men so numerous that she was unable to name any one as a father.

The decent and upstanding members of the community would have nothing to do with her, having given up on efforts to redeem her from her wanton ways. The little cabin she rented was near town, and the pathway to the door well worn by stealthy feet hurrying to and from secret nocturnal visits.

One day, an insurance salesman happened by the cabin. In the stark light of daytime, the littered, unkempt appearance of the place might have discouraged a modern huckster, but during the lean times in question, the salesman knew that need almost always resulted in a sale, and the number of children present established proof of the need at a glance.

He left some time later, having talked the woman into taking out policies on not only herself, but also on each of the children.

Time passed, as it has a habit of doing. Then, after a while, one of the children—the youngest, I understand—suddenly took sick and died. The poor child went into terrible fits and expired before the doctor could get there.

The neighbors, as much as they had despised the woman, felt pity and sorrow for her loss. They gathered to the home, dug a grave and buried the child.

The woman "took on a sight"—wringing her hands, holding her head and crying and screaming that she could never stand to give her baby up.

After the baby was buried, she got somebody to write a letter to the insurance company for her, telling them about her bad luck and wanting to know if they could do anything for her since she had one of their policies on the child.

The company paid without any questions.

From the day she received the insurance check, the woman began to put on airs. She bought herself a lot of new clothes and began going to meetings any time there was one within walking distance. She would jump up and testify about how the Lord had helped her bear her sorrow after her baby was taken away, and she would sing the songs at the top of her voice, to where anyone near her couldn't be heard at all.

After a few months, when her new clothes had been seen by everyone and had begun to be taken for granted, another of her children suddenly became ill with the same sort of fits, and died—again before the doctor could arrive.

Again the neighbors pitched in to help. They came and buried this second child, and listened to her moans and shrieks and screams.

Again, she had a letter sent to the insurance company, and again they paid. By this time, she was becoming a favorite customer of some stores in town, for she bought expensive clothes, shoes and trappings that they carried mostly for prestige and had a hard time selling to anyone else.

There were only two of her children left now. And very soon, only a matter of weeks later, another child died under the same circumstances!

If the woman had been a more respectable person, and not known far and wide as a loose-morals bawd, the neighbors would have been more concerned and taken a greater interest in the poor children. As it was, they just shook their heads and sighed that the poor little fellows had probably died mainly from neglect and poor care, and were probably better off now that they were out of it.

If foul play was suspected, nobody said anything about it.

Only a few months later, the woman came screaming down the hollow, wringing her hands and crying that her last little child had died the night before.

After the burial, the insurance company sent a final check, and after that, the woman was alone in her cabin, no children to care for and no responsibilities save to herself.

If she had put on airs before, that action increased now.

She soon would hardly speak to her nearest neighbors. She had lots of money, and did not hesitate to spend it on herself.

Although the merchants liked to see her come to their stores, they worried that the other ladies in town would stay away, for none of them would have anything to do with "that woman," as she was called.

One day, a passerby happened by the cabin and heard moaning and groaning coming from inside.

Investigating, the passerby found the woman lying there in bed, twisting in pain, looking as if the very next moment might be her last. Neighbors were quickly called, and the doctor sent for. The physician shook his head.

"She is dying," he said. "She has only a few hours left at most."

That night, the cabin was filled with neighbors who came to set up with the dying woman.

She grew worse by the minute, sweating and suffering greatly with pain.

About midnight, the night stillness was broken by the distant squalling of a cat! The sound came from the far away hills, but grew closer and closer.

In those old days, many folks associated cats with death in some way, so the neighbors looked at one another and drew long breaths and shook their heads.

The sound grew nearer and nearer, and the cat at last came right to the door, letting out those loud squalls every minute, until the hair stood up on the heads of those who heard it. Chill bumps ran up and down many spines.

Someone opened the door to see if they could run the creature off, but it came running right into the room and over to the bed where the woman lay in pain.

The cat, the biggest any of the gathered neighbors had ever seen, was jet black and had yellow eyes.

It ran right to the bedside and rose up, hind feet on the floor and front paws on the bedside, right at the woman's face, and let out the loudest wail of all. The woman opened her eyes and looked at the creature, her eyes great with terror. She screamed once, and breathed her last, dying with the open-eyed terror frozen on her face. In the confusion of the moment, the cat disappeared, and was never seen again. The neighbors puzzled over these strange events for some time.

"I think there was more here than we knew," one man said.

After much deliberation, they decided to dig up the graves of the children and examine the bodies. Upon careful inspection, each little head was found to have a big pin sticking down deep through the soft part of the skull. The woman had killed her children to collect the insurance.

"It was judgement that she died the way she did," a neighbor said.

"That black cat…there was something about it," another said.

"I reckon it was the devil, taking that form to come and get her," a third said.

Nobody disagreed.

THE LEGEND OF CRACKER'S NECK

Near Big Stone Cap, Virginia, there is a small settlement known as Cracker's Neck. According to an old legend, the strange name came from a tragic story of violence and murder in the early wilderness days of the Appalachian territory.

Joash Cracker was a long hunter, from out of North Carolina. As was the custom of his occupation in those times, he would travel through the wilderness ridges and peaks until he found an area teeming with game, then set up camp and remain in that location until he had gained all the furs and hides he would be able to transport back to the settlements.

On his fatal final trip, he took his son along, planning to teach the young man the skills of mountain hunting and living.

They found a suitable site near a big spring, which is known today as Jim Black Gilly Spring, and built a small cabin there. There was plenty of game, and the hunting was great. The Crackers, father and son, enjoyed a bountiful season.

No other people were anywhere in the region, and the Crackers had no need to lock their door. They would simply pull it shut and leave the cabin for days on end as they followed the game trails through the mountain.

Nobody bothered their goods, and nothing disturbed the cabin's contents, until one autumn day.

They returned to the cabin to find its contents in havoc and disarray. The foodstuffs had been broken into; dried meat had been ripped down from its hanger hooks and taken away. Some of the furs had been maimed and torn.

The hunters concluded that the vandal must have been a large bear, and, knowing that the animal might well come back again, they decided that it would be prudent for them to hunt singly, while one of them stayed at the cabin at all times to protect their possessions. One day, the younger Cracker came home to find his father in a great state of agitated excitement.

The elder hunter said he had heard something in the woods—some strange creature that made a weird, wailing cry all around the cabin, an eerie sound that seemed almost human in a wild sort of way. He had never heard such a strange sound, he said, in all his years of hunting wildlife. But try as he may, he had been unable to catch even a quick glimpse of the creature.

For some days, both men remained at home, fearful of leaving the safety of the cabin while some unknown fierce creature roamed the woods.

But after a week, when no further evidence of the creature became apparent, they went back to hunting, taking turns in the woodlands and never leaving the cabin together at the same time.

Through the winter, they piled up many furs and by spring they were almost ready to travel back to the settlements to sell the prizes.

One morning, as they made preparations to leave, the son decided to go out and shoot squirrels for breakfast. There was a large hickory tree some distance down the creek, and the squirrels were thick in its branches.

"I'll go shoot us a mess of squirrels while you pack the other things up," the lad said. "We'll have a good breakfast and then be on our way." The big hickory was about half a mile distant, and, sure enough, it was full of the little bushy-tailed creatures. In no time at all, the son had shot six, plenty and more for a breakfast feast.

Carrying his rifle in one hand and the squirrels in the other, the boy trotted back toward the cabin. Just as he drew within sight of his destination, he saw a strange, hairy man, naked as a newborn babe, running off into the distant trees, carrying something under his long, hairy arm. With horror, the son realized that the object was his father's head!

Young Cracker dropped the squirrels and fell to his knees. He lifted his rifle and fired. The shot went true, and the hairy man fell dead in his tracks.

Running toward the creature, young Cracker came across one of his father's legs! It had been ripped from his body at the hip, with tremendous force, a strength far beyond mere human capacity. The elder Cracker's torso lay a bit farther on, and the head and neck had been twisted from it with that same superhuman power.

Young Cracker buried his father's torn body near the cabin. At first, he feared to even touch the strange, hairy creature brought down by his

shot. At last, however, he dragged the huge body to a nearby ditch and covered it with dirt and rocks.

The hairy man was tall, much taller than any man young Cracker had ever seen, and was muscular and had a thick chest. He had large feet, too, too big for any shoes or moccasins then made. He was certainly no Indian, nor was he any sort of man or nationality that the youth had ever seen or heard about.

After the burials, the young man decided to leave early the following morning. He spent a restless day making preparations for the long trip home. As darkness fell, he began to hear the rustle of leaves in the forest and sense movement around the cabin. During the night, strange shrieks and wails pierced the air with terrifying regularity.

Near dawn, the sounds stopped, and when the young hunter ventured outside, he immediately saw that the hairy man's body had been removed from the shallow grave in the ditch and carried away.

Quickly, he packed up all the furs he could carry on his back, and, taking only his Pa's prized rifle along with his own, he left that terrible place and traveled back to the distant settlements of North Carolina, never to return.

Young Cracker often told the tale of his father's murder and the strange hairy man who used such super strength to kill him.

"Pa risked his neck to go on them hunts," he said, "and I did too. I ain't going back in them wilds again as long as I live."

Settlers who moved from this area into the new Appalachian lands near today's Big Stone Gap remembered the tales and found the decaying cabin the hunters had built. They remembered young Cracker's comment about how his Pa had risked his neck for the wilderness treks, and named the area Cracker's Neck in memory of that early long hunter whose blood had first darkened the fertile soil.

Cracker's grave was never found, however, and neither was any burial site of the strange hairy man who had so savagely killed his victim. There was speculation that the murderer may have been an ape, escaped from some distant settlement, gone back to the wild in the mountains.

But if the old tales are true, as we suspect they are, the strange "huge hairy man" may well have been what is now known as a Sasquatch or Bigfoot, that fabled beast that some say yet roams the earth, wild and primeval, a missing link from the known chain of evolution or a near-extinct species that somehow has managed to survive in an rapidly expanding modern world.

Is a Sasquatch buried at Cracker's Neck?

Perhaps someday, archaeologists may there uncover the near-human bones of a huge bipedal primate, genesis Saskehavas, and prove that the ancient story arose from fact, and that Bigfoot did indeed once roam the forests of Big Stone Gap.

BONES IN THE WOODS

Jack Simms bought the mountain cabin to have a place to get away from it all. The peaceful tall pines that murmured in the evening breeze; the nearby little spring branch that sent a soft serene song of its own as it cascaded over rocks in the small cataract; and the chirping and calling of many birds at sunrise endeared the place to his heart his first night there.

Only a few miles from busy, bustling Kingsport and the high-pressure headaches of his daily work, the cabin offered a haven to which he could escape, leaving his cares, troubles and tensions behind.

He furnished the hideaway with an eye toward both taste and comfort, and, by the time his efforts had been completed, the cabin would have been the envy of almost anyone who knew about it or saw it, although no one did.

Jack was not a highly sociable person and cared little for parties and gatherings of any sort that were not absolutely necessary to his business life.

The trail leading up to the cabin was well hidden by low-growing pine branches, yet remained passable in all but the worst weather, and Jack spent as much time as he could there from the first winter.

During the spring and early summer, much of his time was required by his work, and Jack was unable to spend the hours he would have wished at his private retreat. But in late summer, the pressure slacked off, and he found himself seeking more and more time at the cabin.

One lazy afternoon, as the hot sun burned down on Kingsport's concrete streets and sidewalks, causing heat to reflect back up toward the already-too-warm air of the sky, Jack sat in the cool pine shade of the cabin's porch and gazed out at the woodland that surrounded him.

"I've never explored the woods!" he suddenly thought. "All this time I've owned the cabin…since last fall, nearly a year now…and I have never walked around in those woods!"

And so began a regular routine on each of his visits to the cabin. Jack would spend a few hours walking in the woods around his private hideaway, carefully exploring the forest foot by foot on all sides of his small domain.

It was on his third such walk of exploration that he discovered the bones a hundred yards or so from the cabin's east side, across a gully or draw that apparently carried floodwaters to some distant creek when spring thaws made such action required.

Jack spotted a grove of maples among the pine, stately and dignified, their leaves so dense they cast a near-black shadow on the sunless earth beneath them. He crossed the deep gully and climbed his way up the slope to the maple grove.

It was a lovely spot, cool and dark, carpeted with thick green moss.

Jack moved around one large maple trunk and saw a small bank, like that cut out for one side of a graded roadway, just six feet or so behind the tree. Propped against the bank was what appeared at first glance to be the thin, emaciated figure of a man. Jack moved closer and started to speak.

"Hullo," he began, but then stopped in horror. What he had taken for the figure of a man now revealed itself to be only the remains of one!

It was a human skeleton, bones still connected, the dull white color beginning to turn a dingy gray.

Getting over his first shock at finding the bones, Jack went to them and made a closer inspection. The bones had, apparently, never been buried. Examination seemed to indicate that the skeleton was all that was left of a body that had given up life on that very spot, and been left for countless years undiscovered and untouched. Nothing of clothing or personal effects remained. There were no rings or neck chains, no sign of shoes or other apparel. Jack could see no traces of what might have once been a grave, and observation of the low bank established no remote possibility that the skeleton had "washed out" of the soil due to a recent rain. From all indications, the skeleton had been placed in its position by an unknown hand. No footprints or tracks were visible.

The man's first thought was to go to a telephone and report the finding to the sheriff's office. But that would mean, he realized, dozens of investigators tramping by his cabin and through his private domain. Could it have been murder? Was the poor victim, long forgotten, a missing person from some dim time in the past? Jack quickly reasoned that reporting his find would serve no useful purpose, and decided to simply go get some tools to dig with and bury the bones where he had found them. An hour later, armed with pick and spade, Jack made his way back to the maple grove, ready to dig a shallow grave and deposit the unknown remains into Mother Earth's breast.

The bones were gone!

No trace of the skeleton could he find, although he searched the area carefully. No footprints, no broken twigs or limbs, no upturned pebbles or stones! It was as if the skeleton had simply gotten up and walked away!

Jack puzzled over the strange event for some days, but never confided the strange story to anyone.

Nearly a month later, some two hundred yards to the west of the maple grove, Jack suddenly came upon the skeleton, propped against a spreading beech tree, as if taking a nap or resting from long labors!

For an instant, the man panicked. He almost ran from the scene, but, with an iron will, brought his emotions under control and ventured closer to inspect the gruesome sight.

It was, indeed, a human skeleton, bones connected firmly and tightly.

Jack's face flushed in anger. Who could be moving these bones around like this? Someone must be trying to trick him or frighten him with them.

Determined not to be victim to such a sick joke, Jack went back to the cabin and got a rifle.

Returning to the beech tree, he found the skeleton gone!

It was a week later that he got a glimpse of something moving through the bushes, not far from his front porch. He could not fully see the figure; he only noted the movement of leaves.

Jack grabbed the rifle and raced toward the spot. Peering into the dense woods, he caught a faint glimmer of something white disappearing through the distant trees! "It can't be," he told himself, firmly. "Skeletons can't walk!"

That night, sitting alone in his darkened cabin, he heard a strange click and clatter as something shuffled across the front porch! The following night, there came the click and clatter again, and a rough scratching noise on the cabin door.

Jack grabbed his rifle, and, trembling, opened the door.

The wide, vacant, empty eye sockets of a death's-head skull was suddenly thrust in his face! He got a quick view of the full skeleton, bony fingers outspread as if in supplication, before he slammed the door and grabbed his suddenly tight throat as pains shot across his chest and down his arm.

"Must have been a sudden heart attack," the coroner said, three weeks later, when the body in the cabin was discovered.

"It's strange, though. There doesn't seem to be any sign of heart disease. It's almost as if he died from a sudden shock, as if he was scared to death."

JADE WHETZEL'S WAKE

The hills and hollows, ridges and glens that constitute the side of Bays Mountain known as the Blair's Gap Area hold a secret history of their own, most of it never written down, but passed on as fireside tales known only by family members and close neighbors of the clans that have lived there throughout the memory of all living men.

It was in this region—so filled with rushing freshwater streams and abundant wild game in the days when the first white frontiersmen began to arrive—that attracted settlers, and many a rough-hewn, dirt-floor mountain cabin remains to this day. They are hidden away from the often-used roads and paths and out of sight of modern commuters, who may drive past within mere yards of its location every day and never so much as suspect that such a place could exist. Each such cabin is a mute testimony to its builder's skill and preservative techniques. The main trail from Jonesborough to Rogersville ran through that narrow valley, and early commerce indicated that natural developments would eventually make the route a major highway. Such was not to be, however, for the development of Kingsport sent the stage lines along the easier-to-travel river road and traffic soon diminished to a trickle, leaving the shadowy hollows and vales to shroud their inhabitants in isolation.

A former president is quoted as declaring that all history is "bunk" and Napoleon judged it to be "a fable agreed upon." Recorded history is often inaccurate and so full of deceptions and mistakes that it can scarcely be depended on for the truth. The same may well apply to unwritten yarns passed along from father to son or generation to generation as family tales and traditions. Yet, it is a known fact that settlers were living in the Blair's Gap area even before the arrival of the famed Walker expedition that allegedly "discovered" upper East Tennessee and the territory we now know as Sullivan and Hawkins Counties.

Old families! Older than those listed in books as being "Pioneers" and "Frontiersmen." They gained little glory and no recognition, however, for most of them could not write, and few of them were educated well enough to protect themselves from the latecomers who stole their lands and their futures and their glory with manufactured fame of their own.

Beginning with hunters and trappers, who settled their families in cabins high on the ridges where game could be easily found, the old families often deteriorated with the years into dirt-scrabbling ridge runners, trying desperately to feed a hungry, half-wild horde of children that seemed to increase annually until the cabins and lean-tos were filled to overflowing or the tragedy of dreaded disease thinned their ranks to more manageable numbers. When gardens failed and the game began to move on to lesser-populated slopes, many of these families turned to making illegal whiskey as the only source of income readily available.

Women married young, bore children as rapidly as nature would permit, worked hard and usually died before the age of thirty. The man, left with his passel of young'uns, quickly found another wife to replace the dear departed, and life, such as it was, went on. Half-brothers and half-sisters usually had half-brothers and half-sisters of yet another union added to their ranks. Sometimes men died, as men will do, and the widows married again, adding children with a different family name to the brood, some of whom were no longer related by blood, yet they remained families, and forged bonds of kinship that have lasted through the years. In such an environment, strange things are bound to happen, and those events were often remembered, to be told and retold around the family hearthside—unique, strange and sometimes terrifying events. Such a tale is the story of Jade Whetzel's Wake.

The subject of our story, Jade Whetzel himself, was reportedly considered one of the meanest men in the Blairs Gap community. He had outlived five wives, it was said, and may have found a way to help nature dispose of at least some of them. Whetzel was a known whiskey maker and bootlegger, as were most of his peers, but he was also a cruel, savage, selfish individual who had been seen by witnesses to remove the pennies from a dead corpse's eyes before burial, calmly pocketing the coins and allowing the wide-open, sightless eyes of the dead to stare toward the pine coffin lid throughout eternity.

He had killed at least three men, not counting Indians, and had never been known to darken the door of a meetinghouse or church.

A harsh, violent man, Whetzel was a rough-and-tumble fighter, and had once, it was said, cut the thumbs from the hands of one of his own children simply because the child had reached for and taken a second portion of bread.

At long last, to the secret relief of the community, Jade Whetzel died. The cause of his demise is not known to me, but it matters little today. Suffice it to say that when his time came, unwept and unsung, he went to his doubtful reward.

But even a disliked and unpopular individual like Jade Whetzel required burial. The mountain folk, learning of his demise, invaded the sanctum of his hovel, brought in a pine coffin and prepared to lay his remains to rest. A funeral was planned for the following day, with burial to follow on a nearby hilltop, so a wake had to be held that night.

Not many folk volunteered to set up with the corpse, but even a hated individual such as Whetzel attracted a few brave souls for the duty. Rats had been known to gnaw at the bodies of the newly dead, and such indignities were not to be tolerated, even with the subject under discussion.

Riley D. and Carson C., two young men of the settlement, agreed to set up with the coffin through the long autumn night. No preacher would agree to conduct a funeral for such a flagrant sinner, but the burial, set to be executed by dry-eyed acquaintances, was to be held the following morning.

The pale moon was shrouded by heavy clouds, making the night unusually gloomy and dark. The oil lamp, for they could only find one in the cabin, gave a dim and weak light in the shadow-filled room, making each corner seem eerie and forbidding. The shadows seemed to host strange spiritual devils and demons of the dark, whispering to each other, of awful and horrible things soon to take place.

Riley and Carson, brave young men both, sat in the gloom-filled cabin and talked.

"I've heard it said that the Devil Himself will have to come and get Whetzel," he told Carson. "Whetzel was too mean to go to hell by himself. If the Devil wants him, he will have to come in here and get him."

"That's what I heard, too," Carson agreed.

"They say the whole earth will shake when He comes, too."

At that precise moment, the earth suddenly began to shake!

A roar, like that of a mighty freight train, sounded from outside the dwelling, and the doors, both front and back, suddenly flew open.

Riley was looking at the closed pine coffin when the strange sound started, and saw the lid actually lift into the air for a second before it crashed back down on the cold, still corpse.

The entire cabin shook. Windows rattled, and logs creaked and groaned. The floors vibrated, as though an unseen giant had suddenly stomped across and through, and a chilling, terrifying wave flooded up the backs of the two young men, from the base of their spines to the nape of their necks, leaving them frozen to their chairs as if paralyzed.

Then it was over, as suddenly as it had begun, and the night was calm and still as before.

Riley and Carson looked at each other in fear and puzzlement. Neither of them had even had time to run, although the terror that had so suddenly gripped both of their hearts would have forced them to do so had they been able to get to their feet and make their legs work.

Screwing up their courage, they went together to the casket of rough pine boards and lifted the lid, fearfully gazing inside.

Jade Whetzel's body was still there, but the deep-worn wrinkles and lines of cruelty and determination in the dead man's face had changed and rearranged themselves into an expression of horror and fear. The terrified, wide-open eyes of the corpse had lost their pennies, and now gazed out on eternity with dread and awe.

Was it an earth tremor? A sudden, strong wind that simply rocked the little cabin and blew open the doors to shake and jar the sawhorse trestle upon which the coffin rested? Did an underground cave, somewhere in the limestone land beneath the structure, suddenly collapse and fill in?

Or did the "Devil Himself" come for Jade Whetzel?

Riley and Carson never found out. But neither of them ever managed to tell the strange tale without trembling voices and shaky hands.

THEY ARE OUT THERE

I know they are out there. Pa says it is just the wind in the trees around this old house or maybe the creaking and groaning of the walls themselves as they settle down on the old foundations.

He even tried to tell me it could be rats or squirrels scampering around over the roof and in the attic, but he doesn't really know. He hasn't heard them like I have.

We moved to this old house after Ma left.

Pa grew up here. In fact, he says he was born right here in this house, and it has always been home to him.

Not me. This could never be *my* home.

I admit that it is a little better than when we first came here. We got the waterline put in, as well as the septic tank for the indoor toilet and got it hooked up and all. It's better than it was at first, when you had to go outside.

There's water in the kitchen, too, and I don't have to carry buckets from the well any more, but there's still a lot of work to do, like chopping wood for the fires and other chores. It's not at all like living in the city, like we used to do.

Don't misunderstand. I don't mind the work, or even being cold all the time.

What bothers me are the voices. Right outside my window every night.

At first, when I heard them, I thought *somebody* was out there. I would get up and peek out the window, but nobody was ever where I could see them.

Sometimes I can almost make out the words they are saying. I think they are talking about me.

Pa said maybe I heard the sound of a radio or TV set from some neighbor's house, sort of drifting in on the breeze. But that wasn't it at all. They were *talking* about things.

There's a soft voice, like a woman, kind of whispery and sweet, with a sort of sad, melancholy note hinting of tears. And there's the deep hushed rumble of a man's voice, kind of sorrowing, yet firm, demanding, sort of. I wish I could tell what they are saying.

The other night, when the moon was full and it was as bright as a cloudy day outside, I heard them so clear that it was just like they were in this room with me. I still couldn't make out the words they were saying, because it seemed to be some kind of foreign talk I didn't know, but it was words, all right.

It seemed sort of like the man's voice was telling about something he was going to do, and the woman's voice was sort of pleading with him not to do it. I don't know for sure just what they said, but that's the feeling I got.

I got up and looked out the window, even put my head outside and took a good look all around, but nobody was there. For a long time, I could hear them talking, and it seemed like the woman's voice was sort of crying softly.

Old Granny Higgins, who lives up the holler from us, told me that a Frenchman and his wife lived here one time way back before the War Between the States. She said the man came home one day and accused his wife of having a lover. He made her talk a long time, Granny said, and then he killed her and then hung himself, and he died, too.

Pa just snorted when I told him about what she had said, and laughed at me. He says "there ain't no sich thing as haints," and Pa don't lie. I know that he believes what he says is so, but I hear this talking, and it won't go away.

Something's out there.

IT WAITS FOR YOU

By the time he got home, the boy was trembling with terror. Huge droplets of cold sweat, running in rivulets down his face and neck, emphasized the paleness of his quaking flesh. His knees knocked and his hands shook so bad he could scarcely use them for a simple task like opening the door latch.

Fumbling with frustration, he tried to knock, but made only a faint scratching sound. Strength seemed to have left his entire body, leaving him weak and jittery. Ma heard the hushed sound and opened the door.

"Willie!" she exclaimed. "What on earth is wrong?"

The boy stumbled through the doorway and cringed against a wall. "I seen it, Ma," he gasped, in a choking voice. "I seen it jist as plain as day!"

"Oh, Lord!" his Ma replied, slamming and bolting the heavy door. "Same place?"

"Yes'um, right out there on Kincheloe's Curve, on the Lovelace Road."

With gentle words and a tender hand, the woman led her boy away from the wall and got him seated in a chair. He continued to tremble and shake, and she got a blanket to wrap about him.

"Try and put it out of your mind," she said, bringing him a cup of steaming broth.

"I can't Ma. I seen it. It was *there*!"

Through the night the youngster sat, terrified eyes wide and staring, jumping at each slight sound or creaking groan the old house made.

What he had just seen was the Lovelace Road Ghost, an apparition reported many a generation ago. According to the tale, the apparition appeared on certain moonlit nights when the inky black shadows of the scrub bushes and trees along the white-slate ground of the road banks were sharp and clearly defined, and the wind rustled in the autumn leaves where distant pale limbs of leafless trees shown white like skeletal remains.

You could read a newspaper by such bright moonlight, at least the headlines, and all the star-filled canopy of heaven seemed to concentrate its combined brightness on the white ribbon of the road.

In those days, the road ran a series of ridges, dipping and climbing across the feet of the foothills, tall slate banks on each side of the road on the higher grades and frequent dry-wash runs between, like a giant washboard tossed carelessly aside.

Kincheloe's Curve, a dark and forbidding hollow, was shrouded by a dense growth of sycamore and cedar, white-bleached limbs of the former looking like dead men's bones in the eerie moonshine and the squat black shapes of the latter capable of concealing untold monsters of horror from the most discerning, if nervous, eye.

On such nights, when a lone traveler approached the curve, his shoes crunching on the slate gravel roadbed, the apparition was said to sometimes appear. A long, black, box-like shape about seven by three by two feet would seem to slide out from one side of the road.

Cautiously approaching, the wary traveler might, by careful observation, make out the box to be an old-fashioned, homemade coffin. Invariably, the traveler would cross to the far side of the roadway in an attempt to pass the object at the most distant point.

Slowly, almost undiscernibly, the box would slide across the road, blocking the traveler's way!

If the frightened pedestrian tried to dart across the road to the opposite side, the strange shadowy shape would move again, determinedly blocking his way.

Timid souls often took to their heels and left the roadway to go thrashing through the brambles, briars and brush along the mountainside until they were a good distance clear of Kincheloe's Curve. A few brave folk who dared to persist in their efforts to pass found that the coffin shape would only disappear if they walked up to it and peered inside.

The ghastly face of a corpse, eyes open and staring into nothingness, looked back at them. And in the horror of the sight, one who would dare to be so bold saw a mirror-like reflection of his own face. The gruesome specter then faded from sight, leaving the moonlit road calm and serene in the still of the night. A number of such sightings were reported, some by men known to be truthful and bold. "It's a spirit message," folks said, "to remind us of our mortality. The coffin is saying that death comes to us all. No matter who you are, it is waiting."

"It is waiting for *you*."

Time and progress have changed things. Kincheloe's Curve is no more, having been excavated, cleared and straightened when much-needed road improvements were made following World War II. The dips and hills of the washboard roadway are gone and pavement covers the slate bed like a long, dark ribbon of tar.

No one has reported seeing the apparition for many years.

But even today, few people dare walk alone on the road when the bright moon lights the fields like a darkened day and distant winds rustle autumn leaves.

They know it is still waiting.

Waiting for you.

BY DAWN'S GRAY LIGHT

Traditionally, twelve o'clock midnight is considered to be the witching hour, when ghosts walk and spirits moan, filling the night with shrieks, sighs and sounds unholy. That may be just another assumption, another of those things everybody knows that just isn't true.

Ghosts can and do appear at any hour day or night. Just as many sightings have occurred during daylight hours rather than after dark.

Besides, the constant semiannual changes in our clocks, forward and rearward from normal time to daylight savings and back again, have so confused those few ghosts who work the midnight-hour shift that they scarcely know anymore when to make their appearances. As it is, their calls may come at 11:00 p.m., when most folks are either asleep or watching the eleven o'clock news on TV and so ignore the horrifying apparitions because they have enough horror already within view, or, with the inability of ghosts to pinpoint accurate timing, the appearance may come as late at 1:00 a.m., when most people are asleep and don't see them anyway.

So much confusion has arisen over it all that most ghosts have thrown up their spectral hands in disgust and now disregard their assigned appearance schedule completely, relying on off-the-cuff, ad-libbed appearances to achieve their individual quota of fright.

The original purpose of a ghost was to create fright, and thus put more adrenalin into the human bloodstream, creating energy that helped to subdue and replenish the earth.

But modern society, with its rapid communications, has created a rival system that has nearly nullified the effect of the original arrangement. Daily television reports such horrors, perils, hazards and risks for the entire world that few persons can remain unaffected and the constant amounts of fear and adrenaline being added to the already-abundant supply is really more than is needed or can currently be used.

You may pass a dozen ghosts a day, in busy times, without ever realizing who or what they are. They frequent shopping malls, for they like the gloomy, artificial lights of the indoors and enjoy seeing the pained expressions on the faces of shoppers when they look at the prices of items.

They drive cars, ghostly models of all sorts and are often met or passed on both busy highways and lonely country roads.

How often has a car come up behind yours, as if out of nowhere, and whipped around your vehicle to go roaring around a turn ahead and is lost from both sight and sound within seconds? Or what about the slow-moving vehicle you tried to pass for miles on a country road, only to lose sight of it completely after you finally achieved your goal? These, and others, may have been ghosts.

Some specters are late risers and often cannot get up and around until very late in the morning or even early in the afternoon. And among ghosts, just as among human beings, there are night persons and morning persons, a fact which explains the wide variety in ghostly sighting times.

Extensive research has indicated that actually the most likely time to see a ghost is just before sunrise in dawn's early light. It is at this particular time that both the late, carousing ghosts who have been wafting around all during the night and the early-rising ghosts, anxious to be about their busy day's activities, are both out and about. Thus there are two entire groups of ghosts on hand at the particular instance of pre-sunrise—probably the only time in any given twenty-four-hour period that such abundance may occur.

Superstitious persons are still convinced that ghosts are dead people, and live in terror of them. This, of course, is an ignorant and misguided conclusion. Ghosts are merely the *essence* of dead people—the spirit, the memory force, the impression left on this world by the dearly dispatched, demised, departed. As a comparison, a ghost is to a person what a bullion cube is to a porterhouse steak. There is little to get your teeth into, and not much to think about nor digest. The essence, however, is there.

It is in those early minutes of dawn, when dark shadows of night blend into the gray mists of fog, few lamps are lit and the busy activity of the day has yet to begin—such times as these have grown to be the most likely for sighting ghosts.

Many an early riser, making their way through the dark to a parked car, has heard the rustle of movement or felt the unseen presence of *something* nearby.

Thinking it a cat, perhaps, or a prowling dog or opossum, the hurried human pays little attention and thereby misses a rare opportunity at ghost sighting.

Some, however, *are* sighted and recognized for what they are, even if the intended witness has not the sophistication to realize that ghosts are merely harmless reflections of images frozen in time.

In short, some people still not only believe in ghosts, they are terrified of them.

That's how it was with Joe Deacons.

Having reached his sixties with reasonably good health, Joe decided to fight a tendency of being overweight by the unhurried exercise of a daily walk.

The Kingsport area is fortunate to have a number of fine areas for walking, and one of the most popular is the Riverfront Park on Netherland Inn Road.

From the conflux point of the Holston River where Northfork and Southfork come together to form one stream to the old Kingsport Ice House at the opposite end of the park, a paved footpath runs the distance of two full miles. By parking his car in parking lots near either end or the center, a walker can make the full circuit of four miles, from Confluence Point to Ice House and back, with little to hamper his peace or serenity.

Joe began making the daily walks in the early spring, as soon as the biting winds of winter moderated and faithfully continued them until the present instance. Of late, the sweltering, muggy weather has made it difficult to walk during sunlight hours, so Joe fell into the habit of rising very early and taking his walk before the sun rose in the rosy eastern sky.

As the sweaty discomfort from the muggy morning heat increased, Joe moved back his starting time until he began making the early morning walk in that predawn time that is somewhere between night and day and does not fully belong to either one. It is just such times, as we pointed out earlier, that ghosts are more frequent than at any other hour on the clock.

Nelson Sterne had been dead for forty years, and Joe Deacons knew it.

Joe had, in fact, been one of the pallbearers at that long-ago funeral, when his childhood friend had been carried to the awaiting, open grave.

For forty years, more or less, Nelson Sterne had been a seldom-thought-of memory, a fellow pilgrim in the distant past who had stopped off along the long, long highway of life to remain only as a dim recollection from days of yore.

Handsome Nelson—admired by the girls and envied by the boys for his dark, wavy hair and deep-set, expressive, dark-lashed eyes.

Jealousy had been the motive, Joe realized now. That heart-eating emotion was what had caused him to tell Thor Jinson that Nelson and Thor's wife, Irene, were lovers.

Joe had expected that the muscular Thor would give Nelson a sound, if undeserved, beating because of the blatant lie, but the big man had overreacted.

The enraged Thor, not waiting to prove or disprove the false claim, found a gun and shot the unfortunate Nelson, killing him instantly. The law had taken its course and Thor had long since died in prison, serving a life term for the cold-blooded murder.

It was Joe's lie that ruined both of these lives, but that fact never came to light, and lay buried deep only in Joe's memory and the long and distant past. He'd never told anyone about it, nor had he even so much as admitted the truth to himself, but had become convinced, with much self-persuasion, that Thor had acted on his own, and that the lie that started it all was not really a factor.

Joe never lied again; one must credit him with that. The tragedy he had caused came so near to involving and wrecking his own life that he straightened out his morals, bore down to a stern code of ideals and became a respected, well-thought-of citizen.

But truth, like terror, lies always close at hand, and the great awakening light of realization can induce it to rise at an instant's impulse.

It was just such an instant that gray foggy morning that Nelson Sterne's ghost walked out of the mist and reached a hand out to Joe Deacons.

"Joe!" the specter said.

Had the floodgates at Fort Henry Dam not been opened that morning, there is a chance that Joe Deacons might have made it. The lack of rain during the summer had left the water tables very low, and the river was less than waist deep in almost every place, save for a few deep cuts and holes.

But the floodgates had been opened, to let more water down to thirsty Cherokee Lake, and the river was a bit deeper than it might otherwise have been.

Joe's body was recovered from the Ridgefields side of the river, caught on underbrush in a deep hole near the channel.

"Can't understand why he was trying to swim the river, fully clothed," one of the lifesaving crew members said to another. "Looks like he just jumped right in, shoes and all, and started to swim across."

"Could he have fallen in?" another crewman asked.

"I don't think so," said his mate. "There wasn't any place on the bank to indicate anything like that at all. I think he just jumped in, like he was trying to get away from something."

Jason Sterne, home for the weekend from classes at the University of Tennessee, stepped out of the shower, drying off with a large bath towel.

"It was strange, Granpa," he said. "That old man just jumped in the river and started swimming across. All I did was hold up my hand and say 'hello' to him, and he acted like he was scared to death. Do I look that scary or mean?"

"Probably just a crazy wino," his Granpa said. "Don't worry about it. And as far as looks go, you're a fine-looking, handsome boy. In fact, you look just like my brother Nelson looked. And he was the handsomest man in town."

BILL HANKINS'S HAND

Here's a tale we heard that may give you something to think about. We can't say that it is true, or that it even ever happened, for there is no proof nor can any records be found to bear any of it out. But folks in the valley still tell this yarn, and claim that it is true.

They say that Bill Hankins was a strong man.

He had trained as a blacksmith in his youth, drifted into horse trading and when the Civil War tore through the South, Bill had been living in the Carter's Valley section of Hawkins County for a few years, making his fortune by his sharp ability as a livestock dealer.

He was known as a wealthy man, a man who always kept plenty of cash on hand just in case he found an opportunity to pick up a bargain—he could double his investment in short order.

So when the Rebels rode over the ridge that night, looking for livestock, foodstuffs, money or anything else they could pry loose on their current raid, Bill Hankins was their natural target.

They surrounded the house and battered in the door. Hankins tried to resist, but with ten-to-one odds against him, the raiders quickly overpowered the big man.

They tied him securely and propped him in a chair. Then, they proceeded to try and make him tell them where his money was hidden.

Hankins knew his livestock was gone because it would be impossible for him to stand against the armed men who had taken them captive. He knew also that they would take his food supply and any other valuables they could find in a complete search of the house. But the big man vowed that he would not tell about his hidden little hoard of money, which, of course, he would desperately need to get back on his feet if he survived the night of terror they were inflicting.

The Rebels tried slapping him around. They tried hitting him in the stomach, hoping to beat the information out of him. Then they settled down to some serious questioning, using a hot poker and a sharp knife as powerful persuaders.

"If you don't tell us where the money is, I'm going to cut off your hand," the Rebel leader declared.

"Cut-away, damn you!" Hankins roared back. "But if you do, I vow that you will die by that very hand you cut away!"

Two men held his body and two more held his arm while the bearded leader chopped down with all his might against the big man's tough, brawny wrist. It took a number of vicious hacks and some determined sawing, but he cut through the thick wrist and severed the joint, slicing through artery, tendon and flesh like he was chopping down a stubborn cedar tree. Bill Hankins's hand was off.

The blood spurted for several feet. With no mercy in their hearts, the raiders stood and watched the big man bleed to death, refusing to even apply a tourniquet to stop the gushing flow of crimson blood.

In disgust, they let Hankins's body slip to the floor, looted the house for what few treasures they could find and set fire to it as they left. The severed hand was thrown outside in a ditch beside the roadway.

In the gray light of dawn, as the raiders pulled up to rest near the winding Holston River, the leader complained of a choking sensation around his throat.

"There's nothing there, but I feel almost like somebody is choking me!" he told his companions.

They stopped to build a fire and take a rest. An hour later, one of the men discovered that the leader was dead, apparently having choked to death on a bit of jerky beef he was trying to swallow!

A second man died as they attempted to cross the river just north of what is now known as Phipps Bend. The water was only about eight feet deep but some unseen force seemed to pull him from his swimming horse to drown in the swift-flowing current.

One by one the others died, legend says, until a lone survivor was left to tell the gruesome tale of that night's grisly work. It was reported that he died a few days later, supposedly choking to death on a chicken bone.

Since that time, there have been tales of Bill Hankins's hand in and around the long sweep of Carter's Valley. Around the burned-out site of the old house where Bill Hankins once lived, people walk rapidly past the area on dark, gloomy nights.

A few brave souls who have tried to spend any length of time nearby have reported that they have felt the touch of a hand on their shoulder or arm. Nobody so far has stayed around long enough to find out if the hand is visible or is attached to an arm.

It is only a legend, a ghost tale from our East Tennessee hills. Perhaps it is only the prickling of the scalp that is caused by the wind or the fresh air blowing down from the cool ridges that people have felt.

Perhaps it is only imagination, or superstition, or fear. But one thing is unexplained. Bill Hankins's hand was never found. And some folks say he still has a hand in the doings around Carter's Valley.

ANCESTRAL HOME

From a manuscript found in 1926 in an old home near the Kingsport suburb of Sullivan Gardens. The writer is unknown.

I don't know how much more of this I can stand. I've always considered myself a modern, free-thinking, broad-minded person, willing to accept new ideas and different points of view, and my educational background is nothing to be ashamed of. I earned two college degrees, and have continued to be well-read and informed, a modern thinking individual in this modern group-effort world, apart and yet a part of the masses.

I have never believed in supernatural nonsense, nor curses, nor the occult and other such balderdash, and I certainly have never accepted as possible any of the local old wives tales about ghosts, which can be nothing more than figments of the imagination or reflections and shadows that frighten a weak mind.

Yet, there is something strange about his old house, something real and terrible that defies logical explanation and seems to create even a physical reaction from my body itself, completely apart from my mind.

I purchased the old house on a whim, simply because it once belonged to an ancestor of mine.

That was more than a hundred and fifty years ago, before the family lost their fortune and fell from grace insofar as society and prominence in the area is concerned.

That terrible war between the states wrecked my family's fortunes, lost to them their lands and properties, including the vast number of servants

they had gained through diligence and careful management, not to mention hard work.

The main house was destroyed long ago, along with the dormitory-like servants quarters and other outbuildings, in a devastating fire, set by enemies bent on destruction and death which stemmed from jealousy and hate.

As a result of this staggering loss, my poor ancestor was forced to flee the countryside, and leave behind the shattered remnants of his one-time plutocratic estates. In fact, family traditions have it, he was fortunate to be able to escape with his life, for those who rose against him were determined to see his end.

Escape he did, however, and made his way to a large city, where he worked at menial tasks and toilsome labor to eke out an existence for himself and his little family until such time as he might be able to return to the estates and wealth that were rightfully his.

That day, alas, never came.

Unable to gain surplus wealth ample to achieve his goals, the unfortunate outcast lived out his short span of years a broken and regretful man.

His son, in turn, tried to rebuild the family fortunes, but without much greater success. Times were hard, and both money and opportunity scarce. But he was able, by sacrifice and pinch-penny skimping, to educate his son at a fine university.

Because monetary success often clings to those who gain sheepskin-parchments and other such accredited bits of paper, the third generation distant from my tragic ancestor began to rebuild wealth and prominence for himself and his family and aided by careful investments made on the recommendation of friends [nowadays often called insider trading] he regained much of the position that had been earlier lost.

A couple more generations added greater wealth and prestige to our holdings, and by my time, our family's wealth and position perhaps surpassed that which had been lost so long ago.

We had never returned to the ancestral grounds, regretfully, for more attractive opportunities seemed to present themselves in other places.

On receiving my own inheritance, however, I determined to move South again, and to re-locate our family name, by my own presence, as near to the old family holding as possible, and to attempt, through careful maneuvers, to regain at least a part of what had been my ancestors estates.

As I said earlier, the main house and its surrounding buildings had long ago fallen victim to a raging fire, and nothing of them, not even a local memory, remained.

One old house, however, a house my ancestor had built and lived in before he moved to his magnificent estate-house, continued to stand.

Made of hand-formed brick, baked on the site by a hundred sweating workmen, the old house had fallen into ill repair and disuse. Its last tenant or owner, a heart-broken widower who made no repairs, had allowed it to deteriorate to such an extent I almost despaired at the Herculean task of making it once again habitable.

But I was determined, and was able to purchase the building and its small acreage at reasonable cost, moreover, perhaps, because its terrible condition made it extremely unlikely that anyone else would even consider an attempt at rebuilding, which led the owner to price it in accordance to the value of its acreage alone.

Having achieved my goal of purchasing at least a small part of the property once lost by my ancestor, I brought in expert workmen for repairs and remodeling, and within a short span of months, had the old house in modern, livable condition once again.

New wiring, roofing, flooring and wall-paneling had been added, as had a modern kitchen and two baths, and decayed, missing brick as well as rotting wood had been replaced and repaired to make the house livable indeed.

Central heating and cooling and other modern conveniences had been included, installed cleverly in unneeded portions of the original structure to conceal their existence and leave the entire house as much of its antiquity and original charm as possible.

All in all, I was well satisfied with the project, and estimated that I could even sell the property at a handsome profit, should I ever decide to do so.

With a great deal of pride and personal satisfaction, I moved into the house, my permanent abode, I thought, and set about making myself a regular member of the community.

But the people, usually open and friendly, seemed to have a strange mistrust of me, and a stand-offish attitude that excluded me from their local society.

Ridiculous! I told myself.

I, a man with friends on two continents, companion and confidant to some of the nations most rich and powerful leaders, the trusted advisor to men who make decisions that shake the world to its very foundations, find that I am shut out of this local, primitive, clannish, companionship of local residents.

But it was so. They were polite, they spoke when spoken to, or replied when I spoke to them. They answered my questions and courteously filled my order at the local stores, but they made it very clear, by their very politeness that I was, and would always be, an outsider. Thus rebuffed in my efforts to fulfill my plan of regaining what my ancestor had lost, I spent more and more time inside my magnificently remodeled house. I extended invitation after invitation to those persons I came in contact with at the local stores, government offices or other businesses, to visit my home and see what my efforts had accomplished, but none ever accepted. They were all eager to hear my comments and descriptions of work I had done on the structure, and seemed filled with curiosity and desire, but no one sat foot across my threshold.

It was as if they burned with desire to see what was inside my house, but were engulfed with a greater flame of fear which prevented them from coming to bear personal witness.

And thus it was that I became isolated within a friendly community, a lone and lonely man, forced to keep company with two cats and not much else.

It was shortly after these events took place that I first heard the mysterious sound of clanking chains.

I had retired, and was reading a selected volume from my library when the noise attracted my attention.

At first, I had the sudden wild thought that one of my shy neighbors had found the courage to enter my house, and was carrying a heavy chain of some sort, for reasons I failed to understand.

Upon instant reflection, however, I realized this was highly improbable.

It is a trick of the wind, I told myself.

Some farmer is taking his log chain home, dragging part of its length behind him, and the sounds have carried through my door and up the stairwell as though they came from a presence in the house.

But then the chain-sound began climbing my stairs, tediously and tiredly, as if the maker of the sounds was greatly weary from long and hard physical exertion.

I confess to a moment of panic at the startling and unexpected sound.

But I have never been a cowardly man, and I leaped out of my bed and raced to the door, throwing it open wide to observe who or what this unexpected guest, arriving uninvited at this strange hour of the night, could be.

Nothing was there.

There was no visitor, no chains, no presence of any kind on the stairsteps, although I had distinctly heard it only moments earlier, and had been able to clearly identify the location from which the sounds came.

Puzzled over this strange, unexplainable event, I returned to bed and my book, although I admittedly kept an ear cocked for strange sounds for the duration of the night.

It was not until the following night the sounds reoccurred.

Again, I raced to my bedroom door and threw it open, fully expecting to confront the sound-maker, only to find the stairs, once again, void of any presence or personage.

Night after night, the thing occurred.

After numerous tries, I gave up trying to see or catch the soundmaker, and remained in bed when the clanking chains began to move up my staircase.

That time, the sounds continued to the head of the stairs, proceeded down the hallway to a room next door to mine, and then stopped.

I lay in bed, straining to hear, but nothing followed.

Night after night, the clanking chain sound repeated itself.

I suspected rats, brought in the rat-catcher and had the entire house cleared.

The sounds continued, as before.

Could it be a fault in the building? I had workmen in to check the walls (while I carefully examined them, much to the installers puzzlement).

Nothing could be found that would account for the sound of clanking chains.

There is absolutely nothing there, yet I heard the sounds distinctly, night after night.

Although as I stated earlier, I do not believe in the supernatural, nor in ghosts, nor in spirits nor other such nonsense, there is a chill growing around my heart, and an unexplained feeling of panic flooding my mind.

I have come to dread the nightly sounds, and can now face them only with the courage found in a bottle. My health is rapidly failing, my nerves shattered, my brain feverish and restless with a strange and anxious foreboding I cannot explain.

There is something in this house besides me, although I know that cannot be.

There is a presence, unseen and unheard, save for the nightly clanking of chains as it laboriously climbs the stairs, and moves painfully down the hall to the doorway of what may have once been the master bedroom.

What is this horrid, heart-chilling reflection from the past? Can it be an echo of one of my ancestors, restlessly trying to shake the chains of earthly sin and find rest? Can it be the shade of a mistreated servant or other person, locked forever in the agony of bondage, symbolized by the heavy chains?

All of my education and knowledge stands against the sound I hear, and logic and reason are struggling within my mind against uncontrolled panic and terror that seems to grip my very soul.

It cannot be, but it is.

If I live through this night, I shall leave this place tomorrow and then I shall meet…

The manuscript ends abruptly here. The brittle, flimsy pages are yellow with age; the faded ink is still readable, but a dark brown stain has spread across the lower part of the last page.

THE CURSE OF CALVIN KEEN

Not far from our city, in a woodland glade seldom visited by living creatures other than woodland beings, there is a strange little indention in the earth at the top of a creek bank. For all the world it looks like the cave-in of some small animal's burrow, or the collapsed creek bank after a hard spring rain.

There is nothing much unusual about the depression, save for the fact that it cannot be filled.

You can pile brush in it or fill it with dirt, and the very next day, if you go to check it out, the depression will be swept clean, as if a new broom had been energetically applied to its surface.

You can heap up rocks in the depression, filling it to overflow, and, within twenty-four hours, the rocks will all have disappeared as though swallowed by the earth itself.

A trapper who lived in the area once hit upon the idea of setting a steel trap in the depression, hoping to capture whatever it might be that clears the little expanse so diligently. The following day, his traps, stake and all, were gone!

Not many people know the story of this strange little depression, but you will soon know, for I am about to impart the strange facts, in truth, to you.

During the bitter War Between the States, when brother sometimes fought against brother and men died for what was thought to be principle, a man named Calvin Keen lived in our region of the country.

Mr. Keen was a good man, gentle and kind, a man who believed in the teachings of his Lord and his Bible. He could not bear the thought of killing another human being.

A pacifist, we might call Mr. Keen today, but in those bitter days of civil strife, he was simply called "coward!"

You see, Calvin Keen refused to join either the Union army or the Confederacy. He would not fight, he said, on either side, for he felt that fighting and killing were wrong and were no way to settle the dispute that had brought about the great conflict in the first place.

"If any must fight," Calvin Keen said, "Let Jefferson Davis and Abraham Lincoln do it. Let these leaders shed their own blood, not the blood of their fellow men!"

Well, an unpopular political statement like that did not serve to win any friends for Mr. Keen, as you may well imagine. But it did make a lot of enemies for him.

"The man is a cowardly fool," was one of the often-heard comments.

Others were more suspicious. Some Southerners thought that Keen was a spy for the North; many Unionists believed Keen to be an agent for the South. He was mistrusted, hated and feared, yet held in contempt and ridiculed as a weak-willed and characterless man.

Mr. Keen was aware of the opinion his neighbors held of him—he could scarcely help from knowing. Yet, he held his peace, turning away from any confrontation and praying nightly for all his fellow men.

"Forgive them, Lord," he often intoned. "They just don't understand."

One day, while walking through the woodland, Mr. Keen came upon a band of his neighbors, men of the village who had often taunted and ridiculed him in public.

"Good day," he said to them. "God Bless all of you."

"There's that d— coward," Bill Haymes snorted.

"We ought to just string him up!"

And before anyone realized what was going on, that rude and vicious feeling had taken hold of the group, and kindled their hatred of the man who would not fight.

"Let's teach the b—— a lesson!" John Cawlton yelled. "Let's hang him right now!"

Fred Teach grabbed Mr. Keen's arms. Lester Barnes ran and brought a rope from the wagon he had left his horses hitched to at the edge of the woods.

"Neighbors, don't do this evil thing," Calvin Keen pleaded. "I have done harm to no man; I will do none to you. Why will you torment me and threaten my life?"

"Shut up, you cowardly fool!" Bill Haymes said, already tying the rope in a hangman's knot.

The maddened crowd bound Keen's arms to his side and put the noose about his neck.

"Bring him right over here, beside the creek," Joe Leaverton said.

"We'll hang him from that little elm tree there."

The poor man was dragged and pushed to the creek's edge. The loose end of the rope was thrown over a limb of the designated tree.

Together, the angered men pulled on the end of the rope, determined to see an end of the hated individual.

Keen's body rose a few inches, forcing him to stand up on tiptoe, but the elm tree bowed down under the weight of the man's body.

"I'll fix that!" yelled Fred Teach. He picked up a nearby fallen sapling log and propped the tree trunk with it.

"Don't kill me!" Calvin Keen gasped, forcing the words out of his strangled throat. "Stop this now, and I'll forgive all of you!"

"You'll *forgive us?*" Bruce Hayden snorted. "We don't need *your* forgiveness, you coward!"

The sturdier tree held fast, but there was not enough slack to pull the rope tight enough to cut off Keen's breath.

"Wait a minute," John Cawlton roared. "His feet are planted firmly just above a muskrat hole. Let's stomp it down, so it will fall in, and that'll let him fall!"

The men began to stomp the ground around Keen's feet.

"Please, neighbors," Mr. Keen begged, "Don't do this awful thing. If you do, then curse you, may you never be forgiven. May your souls be doomed for as long as a trace of this crime remains!"

"Let him fall!" shouted Fred Teach, as the ground under the unfortunate victim's feet collapsed, and his body jerked with the sudden weight that brought death.

Keen's eyes bulged out of his head, and his tongue lolled out of his gasping mouth; his face turned black and his body trembled in the throes of death.

The gleeful men who hanged him gradually grew more sober and somber, realizing what a terrible thing they had done. They cut his body down and buried it in a hidden grave deep in the woods, hoping that no one would ever know the crime they had done.

A year later, Fred Teach walked by the spot where Keen had died. He noticed the ground was still depressed where the hanging man's feet had stood before the bank was collapsed by the mob's stamping feet.

"That's strange," he said. He piled some rock in the depression, believing it would remain filled. But the next time he was there, the rocks were gone and the depression was just as clear as on the day Keen had died.

Bill Haymes went with him the next time. The depression was again filled, this time with rocks and dirt, and stamped down firmly. But, next day, it was back again, cleared of its fill matter and as distinctive as ever before.

Gradually, all the mob members were brought in on the puzzle, and all of them attempted, singly and together, to fill the little depression on the creek bank where Calvin Keen's feet had stood. In every case, the fill disappeared within one day, and the depression appeared just as before.

Slowly it began to dawn on the men that they were under a curse—the bitter curse of a dying, terribly wronged man.

Bill Haymes grew sick with worry, and hanged himself in his barn.

Fred Teach fell from the roof of his house, which he was attempting to shingle, and broke his neck, dying instantly, the doctor said.

Lester Barnes walked out to see the depression on the creek bank once more, just after Teach's funeral, and suffered a sudden stroke and died there in the woods.

John Cawlton tried to move away from the hollow where he lived, but his wagon turned over going around a steep curve and he was crushed to death in the wreckage.

One by one, all the men involved in Calvin Keen's hanging met untimely, violent deaths, going unforgiven to their moldering graves.

And the little depression on the creek bank remains unfilled to this day, a reminder of the dying curse of Calvin Keen.

THE MAN WHO HATED CATS

Old Man Thompson hated cats. Nobody in the neighborhood ever found out why he hated cats, but, as time went on, it became more and more apparent that Old Man Thompson did, indeed, hate cats. All cats.

His favorite way of showing his hatred for the feline creatures was to slip up on one quietly and cautiously, and pinch its tail between his thumbnail and the sharp fingernail of his middle finger, with a vice-like grip squeezing as if his hand owned the strength of a pair of pliers.

The poor cat would leap into the air, sometimes with all four feet at the same time, and squall loud enough to be heard six city blocks distant. Well, three blocks, anyway.

He would pinch the cat's tail so hard that he would sometimes bring blood right at the tip of the agonized creature's expressive appendage, obviously sending a wave of extreme pain all the way up the animal's spine to flood, in torturous discomfort, the small animal's brain. It was a cruel, mean, inhuman thing to do, and Old Man Thompson loved it.

He would try to surprise cats when they were feeding, nonchalantly enjoying a bowl of cream or a bit of table scraps, by approaching them with extreme caution, carefully and slowly, and reaching out to pinch the creature's tail with a sudden violence that can only be described as vicious. The tortured creature would leap and shriek, screaming with pain as its eyes bulged out of their sockets as if trying to escape the agony from within, while every hair on its back stood up as if electrified.

For a long second or two, Old Man Thompson would hold on to the tail rigid with agony, and then turn it loose, watching as the terrified fur ball bounded away, blindly bouncing off furniture, trees, fences or flower pots in its desperation to escape the torment so suddenly inflicted upon its innocent and unsuspecting caudal vertebra. He would then laugh until he wheezed for breath, gasping like an overheated tea kettle between uproarious and rude chuckles.

Had there been such a thing as a Humane Society in those days, Old Man Thompson would undoubtedly have come to its attention, and found himself facing legal repercussions for his treatment of tabbies, but, since nothing of the kind had been heard of in the neighborhood, the only action against the perpetuator was disapproving looks from some of the ladies and vengeful plotting by children and some of the older boys.

But nothing came of that.

One day, following many months of continuous feline torture, a strange new cat appeared in the neighborhood, and began hanging around the area where Old Man Thompson lived and spent most of his time.

This new cat was large and silver-gray, with short hair and a long, swishing tail that seemed to constantly invite a pinch from the old man's vicious fingers.

The silver-gray cat would appear at the rear of the house, attract Old Man Thompson's attention, and then disappear into the tall grasses and bushes on the adjoining vacant lot, or otherwise fade out of sight by the time the tail-pincher managed to slip around the corner to a favorite spot for launching his surprise attack.

It quickly grew into a daily contest. The silver-gray would appear, then disappear, appear and disappear again, until Old Man Thompson would mutter and curse under his breath as he tried to get close enough to the swishing tail to clamp it in the vice-like grip of his sharp fingernails. Somehow, the cat seemed to always stay just a few feet away from the old man, increasing his determination to new heights and his rage to new lows.

Gradually, as time went on, the cat seemed to stray farther and farther away into the vacant lot next door, and Old Man Thompson cautiously followed, silent as an Indian, careful to not make sudden movements that would disturb the bushes or tall grass.

The taller, thicker bushes toward the center of the lot grew in a massive tangle, almost impenetrable as a mass of thorns and brambles that formed a tight barrier—that's where the silver-gray cat always seemed to go.

Old Man Thompson followed, with the rigid determination of a single-minded despot, cautiously and carefully parting the brambles, briars and bushes to make a narrow passageway for his bulky form.

One day, Old Man Thompson did not come back from the vacant lot. Nobody thought much about it, figuring that perhaps he had crossed the lot and gone out on the other side and went away to visit his daughter or something. But after some days, a neighbor happened to notice that the old man's mailbox was overflowing and that his daily newspapers for the past week were accumulating on the doorstep.

"Old Man Thompson would have stopped his newspaper if he had been going away," the neighbor declared. "He's so tight he wouldn't want to pay for a newspaper he didn't get to read on time."

Other neighbors agreed, but did nothing about a search until one of them noticed that a pension check was among the pieces of mail in the overstuffed postal box.

"That's his check," the neighbor who spotted it declared. "There is no way he would go off and let it just lay there in his mail box. Something's happened to him for sure." Finally, after much discussion, the law was called in and a search effort was made.

In the middle of the overgrown vacant lot, surrounded by thick brush and brambles, the officers found an old, long-forgotten, hand-dug well that had been covered over with boards. The top boards were broken and busted through. A light was brought and shined down into the dark shadows far below, and Old Man Thompson's still form lay there, half submerged in the murky, muddy waters.

When they got the body out, it was found to be covered with scratches and scrapes, raked as if by sharp thorns or claws on face, hands, arms and every uncovered patch of skin.

As the ambulance men carried the stretcher-borne body from the vacant lot, a silver-gray cat came and rubbed around their legs, purring with pleased and happy contentment.

Were the scrapes and scratches on the old man's body made by briars and brambles, or by a vengeful and angry cat?

The mystery was never solved. The silver-gray cat followed the ambulance men to their vehicle, and rubbed about their legs as they loaded their burden. When they drove off in silence, for there was no need for a siren now, the silver-gray cat simply walked down the street and out of the neighborhood, never to be seen again.

EPHRIAM DODD'S CURSE

There was a time when beautiful native chestnut trees grew almost everywhere in our land. The spreading branches of the huge trees provided shelter for both man and beast, the lumber cut from the felled giants built many a home for earlier Americans and the large, tasty, storable nuts provided a considerable part of many people's diet.

The big trees grew from north Georgia to the Canadian border, in fields, forest, villages and towns, prized by all as a God-given gift to Americans, a gift of food and shelter free for the taking.

Early Americans so prized the chestnut trees that they planted them in every town. There was scarcely a village to be found that did not have its share of the shady, spreading trees.

One such giant chestnut tree once stood in Knoxville, Tennessee, at the end of Gay Street, where the railroad tracks pass along the high banks of the Tennessee River, newly formed from the merging of the Holston and the French Broad.

The big tree stood to one side of the end of the busy street, providing a view of the rushing river that passed behind it. Beside the tree, during the bitter Civil War, a gallows tree was erected—tall, grim and threatening.

This fearful object, hateful and gruesome, was used to carry out the orders of the military court, the punishment of death by hanging for deserters and other criminals found to deserve that rash sentence by the court. It was a time of war, and grim and deadly passions flooded the land.

Ephriam Dodd, twenty-four, a handsome, friendly fellow, was born in Kentucky. He migrated to Texas at the young age of eighteen, and soon became a popular young man with many friends.

Dodd's family had been firmly against secession, but young Ephriam, away from home and family, found himself drawn into a company of young men who were enthused about their state's joining the Confederacy.

In those days, a wealthy individual could organize and equip a troop and become its officer. A wealthy sugar planter, Benjamin Franklin Terry, himself a former Kentuckian, joined with a former South Carolina merchant, Thomas S. Lubbock, to equip one of the best outfits in the newly formed Confederate army.

They named the new group "Terry's Texas Rangers," and it became a regiment in the Eighth Texas Cavalry in September, 1861.

The unit quickly became known as a crack mounted regiment, for its volunteers were given the very best horses available and flashy uniforms consisting of blue pants, red shirts, Mexican-style serapes and specially made, wide-brimmed hats embossed with a star and the words "Terry's Texas Rangers."

War is sad; war is bitter.

In their very first engagement, under the command of General Albert Sidney Johnson at Bowling Green, Kentucky, the group's beloved colonel and namesake was killed.

They went on to serve valiantly at Shiloh a few months later, and General Johnson also was killed on the first day of fighting.

The unit was now combined with the Fourth Tennessee Cavalry in July 1862 to form a new brigade under the command of Brigadier General Nathan Bedford Forrest.

Young Dodd witnessed it all, was in the thick of it, in fact. He began keeping a journal, or diary, of events and adventures in December 1862.

Dodd was a devout young man. He spurned liquor and gambling, visited a prayer meeting and bought a number of religious books; these facts were recorded in his little notebook.

Like any other dashing young soldier, he did, however, have an eye for the ladies.

He recorded meeting a number of young ladies, respectfully listing their names as "Miss Maggie Ezzell, Miss Mattie Summers, Miss Fannie Summers, and Miss Mollie Roberts," and others.

Dodd was assigned to duty as a picket for reconnaissance in Kentucky. It was in this capacity that he had the misfortune of having his horse shot out from under him by bushwhackers.

This was in Allen County, Kentucky. Dodd's notebook recorded the calamity briefly, "Bushwhackers attacked us, killed my horse, stampeded all," he wrote. "Came up near Epperson Springs, found the Yanks were there and at Scottsville too strong for us."

The unit made its escape, and Dodd was given a new mount, only to have it stumble and break a leg a few months later. The Rangers were now reassigned to General Longstreet's forces in Tennessee and given picket duty, shielding the main troops from superior Union forces now occupying Knoxville.

Young Dodd missed some of this action, for he was detached from duty to enable him to find another horse. Mounts had become scarce in the Confederate army, and little stock was available from private citizens, most of whom were Union sympathizers.

He at long last found a horse, and bought it for $200, a handsome price in those days.

Heading back to join his Rangers, Dodd and his companions found themselves cut off by massive groups of Federal troops heading north from Chattanooga. This problem was compounded in December when Longstreet abandoned his siege of Knoxville and withdrew his forces from the area.

Dodd's ten-man detail, eager to rejoin their unit, tried to dodge the Yankees by taking a circuitous route southeast of Knoxville. But they ran into a massive Union force, and a skirmish took place. Dodd and two other men, named Alexander and Smith, became separated from the main detachment in a downpour of rain.

Just then, the main body of Rangers came upon a large number of Union cavalry, and made a desperate run for it. Dodd's saddle turned and he lost another horse. Alexander's mount was shot from under him, and Smith, unwilling to abandon his comrades, released his mount. The three men escaped into the woods on foot.

Two desperate days and nights followed, as the trio searched for shelter and aid among a largely unfriendly population. There were a few Confederates scattered around, but most of them were too afraid of retaliation to admit it. They could, after all, lose their property, their freedom, perhaps even their lives for giving aid and comfort to Union enemies.

On December 17, Dodd recorded in his notebook that "this morning the Home Guards got on our tracks and by the aid of Citizens found us."

The trio were taken to the Knoxville jail, where they were given the opportunity to swear an oath of loyalty to the Union in exchange for their release. Alexander took the oath and was released. Smith and Dodd declined to do so, and were locked away in a cell.

Perhaps it was Dodd's notebook that brought about his downfall. When Union authorities examined it, they discovered that many entries referred to the placement of Union pickets, notes natural enough for a scout to record, but one entry stated that Dodd had passed himself off as a Yankee when traveling through Loudon County a few weeks earlier.

That, combined with his colorful clothing, caused suspicions to arise. When captured, Dodd was wearing a Yankee overcoat, apparently liberated from some Union soldier at an earlier date. He also wore blue pants, which he insisted were a part of his regular uniform, but which to examiners looked very much like part of regular Union army equipment. He still had the red shirt and the Mexican serape, and the embossed wide-brimmed hat, but doubts had already begun to grow.

Dodd was accused of being a spy. He denied it, and asked for help from the local Masonic Lodge. Masons came to the jail and pledged to help him, and fully expected the prisoner to be transferred to a Northern prison camp, probably in Ohio, within a few days.

Such was not, however, to be. Dodd was charged with being a spy. Given military trial on January 1, Dodd was under the impression that he had been cleared of the charges, and continued to look for his transfer.

But on January 6, he learned that he was to be hung! His execution, he was told, would take place on the morning of January 8.

When word got out, people in the city of Knoxville were divided over the issue. Many felt that Dodd was innocent, and should be released, while others insisted on his guilt and demanded that he pay the supreme price.

There was a strong feeling that Union officers were seeking revenge for the hanging deaths of Union "bridge-burners" who had been hung just before the blue army captured the city of Knoxville.

The gallows tree beside the river had been used to hang these same unfortunates.

But as late as Thursday night, January 7, a number of people worked and hoped to save Dodd's life. Reverend Joseph H. Martin, of the Second Presbyterian Church, had visited him regularly, as had three Federal chaplains, all of whom firmly protested the young man's innocence.

Through it all, Dodd remained serene. He wrote a letter to relatives, still maintaining his innocence. "I feel prepared to meet my fate as a soldier and firmly rely on God's promises to save the penitent," he told his father and stepmother in Richmond, Kentucky. "Do not grieve for me, my dear parents, for I am leaving a world full of crime and sin for one of perfect bliss."

On Friday morning, a blanket of snow had covered the city. But the Union officials were determined that Dodd's execution take place on schedule.

The prisoner was led from his cell, arms tied behind his back, and placed on top of a wagon, where he was seated on the very coffin he was to be buried in.

At 10:15 am, a detachment of the One Hundredth Ohio and Seventy-fourth Illinois Infantry moved out to the slow and measured beat of a fife and drum detail playing the "Death March."

Slowly the cavalcade moved along Gay Street, which was lined with spectators. Some of the crowd turned away, eyes dimmed with tears, while others watched eagerly.

Dodd sat quietly on his coffin, composed and dignified. He occasionally looked out on the crowd, but usually appeared deep in thought, his eyes cast downward, as though in private, silent prayer.

"I am innocent of this charge," he told Reverend Martin, as he was led from the cell. "I am not a spy."

At the gallows tree, Dodd bravely mounted the steps with his escorts. The noose was placed around his neck and the trap sprung, when, horror of horrors, the rope broke!

Falling in a heap beneath the gallows, Dodd gasped for breath, and struggled to sit up. His neck was badly injured, twisted by the fall, and he was in pain and stunned, but he managed, after a brief rest, to again climb the gallows steps with aid from the soldiers.

Just before the noose, this time a new rope, was again placed around his neck, Dodd looked out at the scene before him.

At his left, the giant old chestnut tree stood, its bare limbs now whitened with glistening snow.

"You are hanging an innocent man," he said, in a low voice. "To prove it, the Chestnut tree will die."

Then the trap was again sprung, and Dodd's life ended.

That spring, the chestnut tree put forth its large green leaves as usual. Blooms appeared, and the surrounding air was soon filled with the pungent odor of chestnut blooms. But a few days later, the blooms fell, and the leaves began to wither. The giant tree began to shed its leaves, as if the autumn season had arrived, and was soon bare and dry.

When examined, the tree was found to be withered, dead and dry. It was cut down for its timber, but the trunk was found to be so full of wormholes and rot that it proved to have no value and had to be burned.

Some people remembered the strange remark Dodd had whispered as he stood on the gallows, and told the story among themselves, and often wondered about it.

The following year, other chestnut trees in Knoxville died as well. Then the plague spread to Maryville, Rutledge and across the state.

Year by year, state by state, the chestnut plague spread until, shortly after the turn of the century, native chestnut trees across the land had died.

Soon, forests all across the nation were dotted with the whitening skeletons of the once-proud giants.

Was it coincidence? Did the chestnut blight just happen to kill and destroy this once-valuable natural resource?

Dodd's prophetic remark that "the chestnut tree will die" was thought at the time to apply only to the giant tree that stood beside his gallows. But the phrase "the chestnut tree" might also have applied to an entire species of the plant.

Is it possible that Ephriam Dodd's death—the horrible hanging of an innocent man—was marked for memory by a power beyond the grave?

THE GRAY GHOST OF NETHERLAND INN ROAD

Hugh H., a Hawkins County resident, visited his sick son in the old building that served as Kingsport's hospital in 1923. Moments after leaving, he died in a car accident on dark, foggy Netherland Inn Road. Is his spirit still warning drivers of this dangerous drive?

"But I saw him!" the frightened young woman kept saying to the puzzled police officer. "He came out from the side of the road, wearing that old-fashioned, long overcoat, and he walked right into the front of my car. I know I ran right over him, or right through him, but there wasn't even the slightest bump when I hit. I didn't feel anything."

Hugh H.'s ghost had been walking along Netherland Inn Road again.

That's not the first time the ghost has been reported. At least five eyewitnesses have told of the man, dressed in old-fashioned, World War I–type clothing, who walks out of the fog on dismal, dark nights and seemingly attempts to flag down their cars to a slower speed.

When the motorist stops, there is no one there. If the driver simply speeds on by, the car runs right through the shade or shadow or whatever the appearance may be.

Who and what is the ghost of Netherland Inn Road?

In 1923, a World War I veteran named Hugh H. (last name unknown) lived in Hawkins County. He wore his old army overcoat one night when he went to what was then the Kingsport Hospital (long since then an apartment building located just across the highway from Riverfront Park).

His son was in the hospital, it is said, and he drove up the narrow, dark river road to visit and check on the youth's condition. On leaving the hospital that night, Hugh H. went out into the darkness of fog and shadow, never realizing that he had a rendezvous with fate just a short distance down the murky road. His car apparently went out of control and he crashed, dying instantly, it is thought, before he reached the Rotherwood Bridge.

Perhaps Hugh H. had been hurrying to get home. Perhaps he had pressed the accelerator down a bit too hard and was driving faster than what may have been safe. Nobody knows for sure but the fact remains that his body was found the following morning in the twisted and crumpled wreck of the automobile he had been driving.

At any rate, a number of drivers have reported seeing a lone, strangely dressed man, holding his hand and arm up to them as though in an appeal to slow down and drive more carefully among the shadows and fog-swept banks of the river-side drive. Whether it is just a trick of the imagination, a reflection of lights on wet bushes or an image from the past—no one seems to know for sure.

But one thing stands out as fact. Those who see, or think they see, the man in the long overcoat on Netherland Inn Road—those who see his arm raised in a warning sign to drive with caution ahead—don't take the offered advice. Not one of them has slowed down yet.

CANEY CREEK FALLS

Haunting Spot in Hawkins County

.If, on a moonlit night in August, you stand quietly near the foot of the Caney Creek Falls—an isolated spot in Hawkins County near the "dividing ridge" between Stone Mountain and Foddershock, on the border of Greene, between the hours of midnight and daybreak—you may strain your ears and hear sounds above the roaring of the cascading waters. Strange noises, like the faint and distant sound of a terrified scream. It seems to come from somewhere up the creek above the brink of the cliff that towers some forty feet.

But don't go looking for trouble. You won't find anyone there. Anyone or anything, save for trees, brush and the rushing mountain stream.

The sounds of the scream have been reported for nearly one hundred years now, and dozens of brave souls have rushed up the craggy bluff to the top of the falls in a vain attempt to find the source of that pitiful and desperate cry, only to meet with the empty stillness that permeates the night air on the mountainside, broken only by the faint tinkle of the rushing waters and the boom of a bullfrog or the cr-r-r-r-e-ead-d-ikit of night insects.

The distant wail of terror is faintly heard in the noise of the waterfall, leaving the listener unsure of its reality, and questioning if their ears are deceiving them or if such a sound actually pierced the solemn night air.

Could it be a nightbird? A rock in the waters, honed to a sharpness that causes the strange faint sound to penetrate the other night sounds of the rushing creek? Or could it be a terrified scream from the distant past, echoing down the corridors of time?

On the fateful night of August 11, 1898, a strange and sudden lightning storm and cloudburst struck the mountainside and valley below in the

vicinity of Caney Creek, creating within minutes the greatest rainfall and most violent winds the residents of the area had ever known.

Lightning flashed, forked and deadly, striking trees and structures alike, bouncing off and rolling like balls of fire across the slopes. Rain, vast like excess water running off a mill dam, came down in a torrent likely unseen since the time of Noah and the Great Flood.

The roar of the storm was tremendous, echoing through the mountain valley and against the topmost ledges, and combined with the vibrating boom of constantly rolling thunder, the terrifying sound brought even the soundest sleeper to full wakefulness instantly.

Water poured across floors on many homes. Loose boards or shutters slammed and banged against clapboard and log wall alike.

In Roe Compton's snug cabin, a short distance up Caney Creek from the waterfalls, the occupants were all quickly aroused.

Roe and his elderly mother were sleeping in one bedroom. Two of his daughters were in the loft above, and his wife and the five other children had been asleep in the other bedroom. The noisy storm shocked them all awake, sending the smaller children rushing to their mother's bed and so frightening the two older girls, Jennie and Ester, that they came hurrying down from the loft to huddle on a pallet between their grandmother's and father's beds.

Compton was already up at the time, having been fully awoken by the very first boom of thunder as lightning struck near the cabin roof.

"It's really a bad storm," he said, trying to reassure the frightened girls, "but it will be over soon."

The older woman, well aware of the hard labor involved in churning buttermilk and making butter, worried about the family's supply of these necessities, stored away in the nearby springhouse. "I'm afraid the milk may be all washed away," she said. The words of this simple conversation were heard by those in the adjoining room.

"Mother," Roe replied, "Don't worry about the milk…"

Just then, a tremendous crash sounded, cutting off the remainder of his words, and followed instantly by a high-pitched, terrified scream.

The entire side of the house burst wide open as a huge pile of logs came smashing through the walls, and the terrified scream, nearly muffled by the roar of the storm and the mad, rushing creek, sounded for a split second before being swept away, down the flood of cascading waters.

The entire room containing Roe, his mother and the two older girls was suddenly gone.

A violent clap of thunder followed immediately, and another resounding crash jarred the house as a mighty tree fell onto the roof, nearly caving it in. The impact sent the battered structure sliding off its foundation in two shattered parts, one collapsing into the maelstrom of waters and the other crashing into a pile of rubble and logs.

By a miracle of fate, the caved-in room that landed on the soggy land side, away from the creek, contained Mrs. Compton and the five younger children. The woman's collarbone was crushed. A heavy log had landed on her chest, pinning her down in the rubble.

The two oldest boys, Johnny and Bird, ages nine and twelve, climbed painfully out of the ruins and began trying to tug the heavy log off their mother. Straining and pulling, they finally managed to free the woman, who, suffering with the broken bone and many cuts and bruises, then helped them pull the other three children from the wreckage.

The mother and children were all bruised and skinned, save for the baby, who had miraculously escaped injury!

Rushing her children to safety away from the creek and wreckage, Mrs. Compton turned in time to see a large pile of logs and drift come washing down the creek like an oncoming express train. It struck the springhouse and then the porch, demolishing both, then swept the remainder of the house from its foundation, down the mountain and over the falls and precipice, forty feet or more.

In pain and desperation, the woman cared as best she could for her youngsters, hoping against hope that, by some additional miracle, her husband and the girls might be yet found, safe and sound.

But such was not to be.

Three of the bodies were found the following day, badly mangled.

The other body was not found until the following Sunday, and was a considerable distance from the scene of the tragedy.

Within seconds, four lives had been lost, a home completely destroyed and the lives of six survivors changed forever.

Some say the terrified scream of the girls, swept away to their deaths by the mighty deluge, can still be heard in the vociferation of the torrent. Others claim it is only the natural sounds of a mountain stream, rushing madly down its rocky slopes.

Only one thing is sure. All admit to feeling cold chills along the spine as the spate of inundation swirls past in the echoing moonlit night.

THE GHOST WHO WAS LONELY

.I was being admitted to the local hospital for a bit of surgery when the nurse asked me about my work.

"I'm a newspaperman," I replied. "Have been for many years, but now, I mostly write feature stories and human interest pieces. Lately," I told her, "I am working on collecting the ghost stories I have written over the years, and I need some new ones. Is this hospital haunted? With all the trauma that goes on here, it well could be."

"No," she said. "I haven't heard about any ghosts here, but I can tell you a lot about the ones in the house where I grew up!"

Well, you don't often hear that kind of statement from a nurse, or any other medical professional, so I asked her to tell me about it.

"It was just an ordinary house," she started.

I grew up there with my mother and father and my sister. It was definitely haunted by a ghost, and we knew who that ghost had to be! It was my twelve-year-old cousin Carl.

Carl was killed by a horse in our front yard, right outside the front door, when the horse kicked him in the head. He was carried inside and died within minutes.

That happened when I was very young, but I remember it well. Right after that, the strange things began to happen. They were all sort of mischievous tricks, really…Just the sort of thing a twelve-year-old boy would do.

We'd hear running footsteps go up the stairs and the commode would flush, but no one was ever there! Lights would go off and on, doors would slam, sometimes clothing would just fall off of the hangers in the closet.

My dad would be taking a shower, and the water would suddenly change from hot to cold. He would yell out, "Who turned the hot water off?" Then it might come back on.

Sometimes, the water would simply stop running, leaving the person who was trying to take a shower all lathered up with soap and no way to wash it off. They would have to get out of the shower and rub it off with a towel, then the water would come back on!

I remember one night, my sister and I slept together in the same bed, we had gone to bed when a light across the room came on.

"Go turn that lamp off," I told her.

"No way," she said. "You go do it."

I got out of bed and went around and across the room and turned the lamp off, and then made my way back to the bed in the dark. As soon as I got under the covers, the light came back on!

"It's your turn," I told my sister, but she still refused. Just as I was starting to get up again, the light went off. Then it came back on. My sister pulled the covers up over her head and squeezed her eyes shut tightly.

"Viv," she said, "I'm scared!"

"Me too," I answered. I snuggled down near her and squeezed my eyes shut also, taking deep breaths but being as quiet and still as I could in my terror. Then the lamp went out and stayed off, at least until I went to sleep.

Throughout my teenage years, the strange happenings and tricks continued. When I graduated high school, I had a couple of weeks at home before I was to leave for college.

One night, just before I left home, my father came to the breakfast table with a strange expression on his face.

"I want all of you to hear this," he said, making sure that my mother, my sister and I were all paying attention. "I don't think Carl will be with us any more. I had a vision…or a dream, whatever it was, last night."

"I think I was awake, I am pretty sure I was, but I saw my Papa standing at the foot of my bed! As you all know, Pop's

been dead for many years. Twenty now, I think. He had a kind of glow about him, and he was smiling.

"Then I saw a smaller figure beside him, holding his hand. It was Carl! He looked just like he did before that horse kicked him and he died. He looked up at Pop with happiness in those big eyes of his and, Pop looked down at him and smiled.

"Then the images both faded away and I realized what had happened. Pop has finally found Carl, and Carl is no longer alone. They are both in heaven and happy."

I left for college the next day, and never did spend much more time at home, but my sister and my parents said they never had any more ghost tricks in the house.

Carl had been lonely, and was trying to get our attention to let us know. So I know about ghosts, having grown up with one. I may not believe all the ghost stories I hear, but I know some of them are true. Mine certainly is!

REBEL'S GHOST AT PINEY FLATS

At least a dozen people have reported hearing the pitiful cries for help that come from a grove of old trees near the crossroads in Piney Flats. A number of times the sound has been investigated, and on at least two occasions a frightened individual has called 911 to report the desperate, urging sound.

But no one has been found, and by the time searchers arrive at the scene, the cries have always stopped.

Could it be just wind in the tall trees, perhaps moving a dead, broken limb against the bark of the tree trunk? Is it possible that fluttering bats, flying out of their cluster to seek night prey, make the mournful sound? Is it an echo from the long-forgotten past, somehow preserved in time to sound faintly again and again as time slips by?

In 1863, a sharp and deadly skirmish took place at that grove of trees between Union and Confederate forces. Several men were killed; soldiers of both armies lay dead and dying in the brush and grass when the shooting stopped.

When the Southern troops slipped away toward Blountville, taking along their dead and wounded, and the Union men, doing likewise, headed back toward Bristol, one man, a Confederate soldier, wounded and bleeding yet alive, was left behind.

"Help me," he begged. "Somebody please come and help me!"

No help came. The soldier died an agonizing death there in a clump of bushes.

Some days later, two local boys passed by with their dog, and discovered the body.

The soldier was given a proper burial in a nearby cemetery and the incident faded into history.

A year later, a local farmer was making his way to a nearby tavern one night when he heard the groaning cry, "Help me, please help me!"

He ran toward the sound, but saw no one. The sound did not come again, and the farmer hurried on to the tavern, where he reported the strange incident. Several men there went back with the farmer to the spot, but found no injured person and heard no more cries for help.

A few months later, however, another passerby reported hearing the call for help.

To this very year, now many decades after the bitter War Between the States ended and hatreds gradually died out, the sound is occasionally heard.

People of Piney Flats say there is nothing to the story—it is just another old country tale. But they walk quickly past the spot if they pass it alone after dark.

THE REVEREND'S GHOST

One of the strangest tales often repeated in the East Tennessee hills may be grounded in historical fact. The story features a ghost reportedly seen by a number of people over a long period of years, sights that came to an end when the balance of justice was set straight and a wrong was corrected.

During the War Between the States, Reverend John A. Bowman was pastor of the little Pleasant Hill Church of the Brethren in Sullivan County. The preacher lived in a log cabin situated beside the church building. Reportedly a good man and a fine preacher, Brother Bowman added many names to the church roles through his efforts and baptisms.

The region was divided in its loyalties between the Union and the Confederacy. Around Bristol, on the Virginia state line, secessionists prevailed. But in other parts of the county, Union sympathizers were in the majority.

Into this confusing mix, Confederate raiders often came sweeping down from Kentucky to loot and steal and to conscript horses, mules and foodstuffs for the grand gray army of the South.

Sometimes they were chased by Union soldiers, who returned from the chase to raid and steal and conscript any remaining horses, mules and foodstuffs.

Word came to Reverend Bowman that Confederate raiders were approaching his church, and would be likely to take anything of value they could discover. The preacher busied himself locking up everything he could find to save from the sure grasp of the motley crew of cutthroats who would one day be honored as daring Dixie Daredevils.

He buried his money, locked up his tools, guns and foodstuffs. He went down to the church and locked it up as tightly as he could for fear that the raiders would carry off the very pews for firewood, which they had reportedly done at other churches.

When he was finished with those tasks, Reverend Bowman went to his barn and locked up the harness and other tack as well as he could, and was in the process of locking his horse away in the barn when the raiders rode up.

The mounted mobsters demanded that Bowman give them the horse. He refused, and was shot down, murdered in cold blood for his refusal.

As further retribution for this independence, Reverend Bowman's cabin was set afire by the raiders, who then took what they could find that remained loose, including the horse. Then they rode away.

A neighbor found the preacher's body the following morning. Examining the wounded preacher, the neighbor thought he felt a faint heartbeat, indicating that Bowman was yet alive. He and others carried the bleeding victim to a newly built corncrib near the barn and did what they could to aid him.

The wound was terminal, however, and Bowman died a few hours later.

The following morning brought a dark and dismal day for April. The neighbors placed Reverend Bowman's poor bloody body in a pine coffin and carried it to the little graveyard near the church, where a hastily dug grave awaited. The gentle April rain fell from blackened skies while they shoveled muddy sod onto the unpainted pine planks of the coffin lid.

For the next hundred years, the ghost of Reverend Bowman was frequently reported as being sighted in various places near his death site or grave. He has been seen by old men, young men, boys, girls, young and old women and by women who refused to tell or admit their age.

Talk grew and grew, and local folk sought for an explanation for the ghost's repetitive appearance.

"Why you reckon that Preacher is a-haunting us for?" Jud Adams asked.

"Why, he's a-tryin' to tell whar he buried his money at," Jim Yonkers said.

"Naw, that ain't it a-tall," Ralph Jones insisted. "He's trying to tell who it was that shot him, so he can get revenge!"

Whatever the reason, the reverend's ghost seemed to continue to be seen from time to time, especially during a dark, dismal April day, such as had been the day he died. It was agreed upon that the reverend seemed to be trying to communicate something to all who saw him.

At long last, when some local folks were engaged in researching church history for the area, they came across a bit of information that could lend a clue. Apparently, Reverend Bowman had been involved in a disagreement with some of the elders of his church and had been defrocked and excommunicated a short time before his death!

Why had the good preacher been so ill treated? Well, he had gone to court and sued a man who had broken an agreement with him.

In those strict, unbending days, the church took literally the admonishment of Paul to "let him have your coat also," and so considered Bowman's action as sinful.

Because of the war, Bowman was unable to travel to Philadelphia to get his name cleared and have the local excommunication overturned.

As it stood, all the people he had baptized and added to the church roles were thus in danger of being excommunicated as well, for they had been brought into the church by an unworthy and unauthorized preacher!

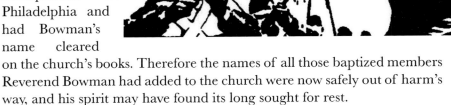

Was that what Bowman's ghost was trying to relate?

A group of churchmen felt that such might be the case. They took the matter to the church's headquarters in Philadelphia and had Bowman's name cleared on the church's books. Therefore the names of all those baptized members Reverend Bowman had added to the church were now safely out of harm's way, and his spirit may have found its long sought for rest.

Reverend Bowman's shade has not been reported seen since.

THE GHOST OF ROTHERWOOD

On the outskirts of Kingsport, Tennessee, where the Holston's two forks come together to form a larger stream, the Rotherwood Plantation mansion graces the hill on the Hawkins County side of the river.

Although much misinformation has been reported concerning the magnificent old residence, a considerable number of individuals have reported certain unexplainable sightings of ethereal images in or near the structure.

Local legend has it that the house was built by early plantation owner Frederick Ross in 1818, but, sadly, such is not the truth. Ross built a mansion, it is true, and named it Rotherwood after a house in Sir Walter's Scott's novel *Ivanhoe* in tribute to his daughter, Rowena, who also was named for a maiden in the story.

But Ross's mansion was situated on top of a hill, some hundred yards from the present building. It was constructed from two houses that Ross had moved to the site. He then had a large ballroom-like center section built between the two structures, joining them into a magnificent manor house.

Unfortunately, the Ross mansion was burned to the ground in the closing days of the Civil War. Whether the destructive blaze was arson, an act of war or an accident has never been established.

By that time, Ross had already given up his attempts to establish a silk manufacturing plant nearby, and has sold his estate to another owner and left the state.

His decision to do so was prompted by two things: the tragic death of his daughter Rowena and the failure of his business establishment.

Rowena was, reports say, a lovely girl, and her father's pride and joy. Immensely wealthy for the time, Ross was influential and powerful throughout the area.

Ivanhoe, his favorite work of fiction, had so impressed him that he named his daughter for one of the novel's major characters, and his plantation from it as well.

In addition to his wide-ranging farming interests, from which Ross shipped large amounts of produce and grains down river on flatboats, the idea came to him that the Holston River country might well be utilized for silkworm cultivation. He imported mulberry trees from Japan and planted a large grove of them.

As soon as the rapidly growing trees took root and thrived, Ross imported silkworm eggs from the far island of the Nipponese.

In the river below his home, in the Northfork stream, Ross had a mill plant constructed to his own specifications, patterned after similar such plants where silk production was successful.

The silkworms at first seemed to thrive in the mulberry trees, and things boded well for the enterprise, but the factors of fate are fickle to all men, rich or poor. The price of cotton fell, increasing its use in clothing manufacture and lowering the price of raw silk. A sudden unexpected winter of bitter cold dropped temperatures to well below zero, freezing the silkworm eggs and making them infertile. Ross grimly bore the loss and planned to order more silkworm eggs the following spring.

His daughter Rowena, in the meantime, had fallen in love with a handsome local youth and had married on a lovely spring day.

Just after the morning ceremony at the Presbyterian Church in the village of Kingsport, Rowena had remarked about the beautiful tree blossoms she had seen on the dogwood trees just across the river, and how lovely they would be for a centerpiece at the dining table.

Gallantly, the groom had volunteered to take a flatboat and row across the steam to fetch a load of the flowering stems.

As the bride, still wearing her wedding gown, watched from the riverbank, her groom's flatboat capsized in mid-stream, and his frantic efforts to swim proved futile. He drowned in the rushing water, while Rowena looked on in horror.

Not long afterward, Rowena's body was found floating face down in the rushing stream.

It was after this tragic death that Ross lost all interest in trying to develop the silk business and sold his entire estate and moved away, never to return.

Although the original Ross house had been destroyed by fire, the new plantation owner had another one constructed that still stands, magnificent and picturesque on the Holston's bank.

A number of individuals have reported seeing a strange sight near the river bank there. The vision of a woman, dressed in a flowing white bridal gown, runs frantically along the shoreline, as if trying to reach or signal to someone in the river. But a brief glimpse is all anyone ever gets before the image vanishes.

Is it Rowena, trying to reach her drowning bridegroom, or is it just a wisp of fog and overactive imagination?

THE FURY OF THE FLIES

According to local legend, Joshua Phipps was known to be a cruel master. Hired to operate the Rotherwood Plantation on the Holston River by its new absentee owners, Phipps was allowed to provide his own labor force, and so brought along a considerable gang of slaves he had purchased for the purpose.

The large plantation, developed by wealthy Frederick Ross, had been purchased by investors after tragic events had caused its founder to lose heart and move to a distant place.

Phipps brought along both male and female slaves, selecting the best-looking women to serve him as cooks, maids and bedfellows, while putting the males among them to work constructing rude cabins for themselves and for Phipps to live in while a new large brick mansion was constructed down the hill from the original site, which was then only a burned-out ruin.

Phipps believed in working his will by force and by lash, and he carried a long blacksnake whip at all times for just such purpose. He also had two loaded side arms buckled at his belt, and had been known to shoot down in cold blood any slave who dared dispute his orders or talk back to him.

Rumors had it that he sometimes impregnated one of the female house servants who had been forced to be his bedfellow, but no mixed-blood child ever survived, for, it was said, Phipps simply smashed in the skull of the newborn babies and fed their little corpses to his hogs!

Hated and feared by all the slaves, Ross continued his reign of terror on the plantation for several years. But time, in its fullness, rolled around, and his time came.

One day, Joshua Phipps awoke with a severe pain in his chest. He could not move. He could not call out. He could not rise or get out of bed. Then, from the open window, a swarm of black flies came rushing in.

They settled on his head and face, covering his entire face and even crawling into his open mouth and his nose!

Gasping for breath and unable to move, Phipps lay there, unloved, unaided and unable to help himself or blow the flies away.

Some time later, one of the servants discovered his cold body, still covered with the swarm of flies! When a neighbor was sent to report the death to local villagers, the flies had been chased away, and Phipps's pale, cold body had been placed in a homemade coffin, such as had been often provided for the slaves.

Although none of them admitted it, the feeling among local citizens was that the slaves had called down a curse on Phipps because of his cruel and harsh handed treatment of them.

Because he was not a churchgoer, Phipps's funeral was held at the newly constructed mansion. As the carriage carrying his casket up the hill to the cemetery moved along, it suddenly stopped, and the wheels refused to turn again.

Confused and troubled by the unmoving carriage, the burial party withdrew aside to decide what action to take. Suddenly, the canopy covering the casket began to move, and a huge black dog leaped out from beneath it and ran across the hillside, a huge swarm of black flies chasing after it, trying to land on its head! The dog's ears were laid back as if in terror, its tail tucked between its hind legs as if in shame and fear.

Fearfully, some of the people approached the carriage, which now rolled along with ease.

When they lifted the coffin to place it in the freshly dug grave, it was strangely light. Phipps had been a large, heavy man, well over six feet tall and weighing nearly two hundred pounds.

Since that day, the large black dog has often been glimpsed along the Rotherwood hillside, eyes wide and red with panic and a thick swarm of black flies streaming after it as it flees in terror.

HOLIDAY OF HORROR

One week before Christmas 1942, with America desperately fighting on two fronts (the Pacific and Europe) in World War II, home folks in East Tennessee were beginning to feel the pinch of war shortages and restrictions.

Gasoline was rationed, as was butter, lard, sugar and many other normal daily needs. Work was available for anyone who wanted a job, for more than one thousand men had been inducted into military service in the Kingsport area alone, and that situation was reflected all across the country.

Many women had moved to towns from farm life to take jobs, replacing the men who were now fighting or training to fight for the just cause of freedom.

Readers who lived through those days will recall blackouts and blackout wardens; shortages of everything; ration stamps; draft notices; star banners in windows, proclaiming that a son or husband was serving his country; and many other details of wartime living.

But in spite of all the difficulties of daily existence in a wartime economy, Christmas came around as usual. It would be a sad and lonely Christmas for many, with loved ones far away, and there would be a lack of joy in many homes. But for children, Christmas still held the charm and excitement it always brings.

Santa would come, the youngsters knew, bringing gifts and toys and goodies. Because of the approaching holiday, the kiddies were on their very best behavior, jumping quickly to do the bidding of their parents and avoiding any fights or squabbles with friends or siblings. And they took responsibility even more seriously than usual.

Such was the case with the Collins and McGhee children, who resided with their parents in modest frame homes on Bridwell Hollow Road, near Cedar Grove School.

That was particularly true of fifteen-year-old Kathleen Collins, who was dependable and reliable as a babysitter and caretaker for her younger, six-year-old brother, Hubert; three-year-old Janice; and fourteen-month-old Hugh McGhee Jr., her beloved niece and nephew.

With school being dismissed for the holidays, Kathleen had ample time to look after the younger children, and enjoyed doing so.

Amos Collins wanted to buy some special gifts for his family. Money was tight, of course, due to living expenses, but when payday rolled around on Thursday, Amos had ample funds to splurge a bit for Christmas. "Let's take the bus and go shopping tomorrow," he told his wife. "We can get toys and gifts for the kids and make it a happy Christmas."

"Kathleen is out of school," his wife said. "She enjoys looking after the younger children. Would it be all right with you if I asked our daughter Beulah and her husband Hugh to come along with us?

"Sure," Amos said. "Kathleen will enjoy having Janice and little Hugh along with Hubert. She can read them stories."

And so a shopping outing was planned.

The Collinses had two married daughters, Beulah and Lottie. Beulah had married Hugh McGhee of Fall Branch, and their union had been blessed with two children: Janice, now three, and little Hugh Jr., who had celebrated his very first birthday just two months earlier. They now lived near the Collinses' home, just next door, in fact. Lottie had married Carl Gilley, and lived nearby as well, just a distance of a mile or so.

The McGhees were delighted to go Christmas shopping with her parents. Hugh, who worked at Mead in Kingsport, had used up his gasoline allotment and so was not able to drive his car.

"We can catch the bus down there on Bloomingdale Pike, just a little way from the house," Mrs. McGhee said. "If Kathleen will stay with the little ones, it will be perfect and I will bring her a pretty if she will."

"You don't have to do that," her mother insisted "Your sister Kathleen is a fine baby setter. She has kept the children many times. After all, she will be sixteen on her birthday, so she is practically grown up. At least she thinks she is. She likes to play school with the children, and pretend that she is the teacher. I can always count on her to be dependable."

"Oh, Ma, I know she is dependable. She has kept my kids for me before now. Why don't she come here and stay at our house with the children?"

Beulah asked. "That way, we can take the toys and things we buy to your house and hide them until Christmas."

And so, on the clear and cold Friday afternoon, December 18, 1942, the four adults, parents and grandparents, told the children to be good, gave them hugs and kisses and left home to catch the one o'clock bus to town.

No written record survives to accurately tell just what happened after that.

It can be assumed from past occurrences that Kathleen played with the children for some time, perhaps gave them a snack, and read a story or two to them, then put them to bed for a late afternoon nap.

She put the two boys, Hubert and Hugh Jr., in the front bedroom and three-year-old Janice, who had already dozed off to sleep, in the back room. The children were all within easy hearing distance in case they should wake up and need her.

After checking the fire in the stove in the front room, as was her usual habit, Kathleen seems to have decided to lie down beside her six-year-old brother, who was a bit frightened to be in a strange room. Then she dozed off, as well, soon drifting off into sound sleep beside Hubert, who was already asleep.

At about 4:00 p.m., Mrs. Iva Broyles, a near neighbor, happened to look outside her door and noticed smoke pouring out through the window casements and door frames of the McGhee home.

"Oh, Lord!" she cried. "Hugh and Beulah's house is on fire!"

Screaming for other neighbors to come quickly, Mrs. Broyles ran to the burning home, but was unable to enter it due to the heat and flames inside. A large group of neighbors quickly gathered at the burning home, hoping to find a way to rescue the suffering victims from the blaze.

They could hear cries and sobs from the poor children who were trapped inside and desperately tried to organize a bucket brigade from the nearby creek to throw water into the intense conflagration.

"Mamma!" they heard a voice call, the faint sound almost lost in the roaring, crackling fire of the dry wood of the frame house.

"Where is Beulah?" said Lottie Gilley, the other Collins daughter, had just arrived, having walked up the road for a visit. She had seen the flames licking out from the roof of the house from nearly a quarter mile away.

"She and Hugh took the bus to town," someone replied. "They have gone Christmas shopping for the children. And Mr. and Mrs. Collins went along with them!"

"Oh, Lord! The children are in there! Does anyone here know which of the kids are in there?"

"Kathleen is in there, looking after them. Your little brother Hubert and Beulah's two, Janice and Hugh, Jr. are all with her," she was told.

In the crowd of anxious onlookers, another neighbor, J.E. Collins, cocked his head to one side. He thought he heard a wail coming from a direction different than the others. On a hunch, he ran around to the rear of the burning dwelling and held his arm in front of his face to ward off the burning heat radiating from the blaze.

Through a window, he caught a glimpse of a tiny girl, frantically pulling at the window seal! Collins ran forward, smashed the window glass and grabbed the girl, thus rescuing the three-year-old, Janice, who would be the only survivor.

As helpless neighbors watched, the flames leaped through the roof and the billowing smoke forced those in the crowd who happened to be too near the building to move back.

The screams and groans were silent now, for the inferno had taken its toll.

"Somebody needs to call the law and get them to try and find Amos and his wife," a neighbor said.

Harvey Mercer ran to his home and telephoned the sheriff's office.

There was not much else to do. With no fire department or equipment to serve the suburban area, fire victims were left pretty much alone to fend for themselves in those days.

Although the City of Kingsport had modern fire equipment, they were not permitted to work outside the city limits, and so could offer no help in such cases.

Within an hour, Amos Collins and Hugh McGhee and their wives had been located. They were told only that they were needed at home, and were driven to the devastating scene by a sheriff's officer.

There is no need to even try to describe the horror, shock and sadness that overcame the brokenhearted bereaved, torn by cruel fate from a merry Christmas shopping spree to the scene of tragedy and horror.

The parents, collapsing in grief, were taken to the home of Mrs. Irvin Nickels beside the destroyed house to receive medical treatment from a physician who has been summoned to come and care for the grief-stricken families.

Highway Patrolman Frank Williams and Deputy Sheriff J.K. Breeding sifted through the rubble of the ash heap that had been a home. They found the ashes of the children in their beds, although the poor little forms had been burned beyond any recognition.

Kathleen's remains were in the bed beside that of her little brother, Hubert. Little Hugh's tiny form was in another bed, identifiable only by size.

On Sunday, December 20, a combined funeral service for the children was held at the Vermont Methodist Church. The ashes of all three had been placed together in a coffin, and they were buried in a single grave that afternoon.

This sad, sad Christmas story had made its impact on the minds and hearts of all who witnessed the conflagration or even looked upon the ash heap that remained after the blaze died out.

At the Collins home, where the distraught parents and grandparents had left the purchases they had made in town, a little paper-wrapped parcel rolled out on the porch as if pushed by an unseen hand.

Wind tore at the wrapping and peeled it back, exposing a shiny new little red wagon, the heart's desire of a six-year-old boy who would never see or play with it.

And to this very day, if you walk past the log house where the Collins family lived on the lot next door, where the McGhee home burned, you may hear the roaring sound of a raging fire, the snap and crackle of the leaping flames and a pitiful, wailing cry.

Is it just the winter wind, whistling down what is now called Forest View Road, mixing with the snap and crackle of the willow twigs along the creek across the road, and the mournful protest of an old screech owl, who often perches in a nearby tree?

Or is it sounds of horror frozen in time?

Visit us at
www.historypress.net
....
This title is also available as an e-book